CELEBRATE

Hardie Grant

BOOKS

To my friends and family, who have always been there
to help celebrate those special moments in our life,
and of course to Bruce, for always being there by my side.

CELEBRATE

Chyka Keebaugh

CONTENTS

WELCOME!

 For as long as I can remember, I have loved setting a beautiful table.

When it comes to celebrations with friends and family, the table is what I visualise first. I spend days making lists, dreaming up floral combinations and planning the perfect menu. I love it; I've always loved it. In an era when we are all so busy, stopping to spoil my family and friends with a meal or gathering is my greatest pleasure.

In this book, I share my interpretation of holidays from around the world, exploring their traditions and putting my own creative spin on these occasions. And, of course, I share a delicious recipe and cocktail (or two) along the way.

In the process of writing this book, I've learned many things about the various cultural traditions and festivities of the world. They are full of layers, excitement and colour, and I am delighted to bring them to life for you here. I hope that the ideas in the following chapters inspire your own special events, whether that's a birthday, an anniversary or a bigger occasion, like Christmas. All that good china hiding away in the back of your cupboard can now be brought into the light – and I'll show you how to use it.

I have tried my hardest to represent all the cultures and traditions in this book as truthfully and respectfully as I can. There are many more themes and occasions that I would have loved to have included. Maybe they're for the next book? Until then, let's relish the joy of having so many wonderful things to celebrate.

To get you in the mood for your celebration, I have created playlists for every chapter in the book. You can find them on Spotify under Chyka Celebrate. Have a great party!

Love,

xx

BIRTHDAY PARTY

A SPECIAL BIRTHDAY LUNCH

" Who doesn't love the idea of celebrating a birthday with a group of friends? On my birthday, I like to celebrate with family, of course. But I also like to gather my closest girlfriends and have a special lunch.

I always enjoy adding an element of surprise for any event, so picking the perfect location is a must. My mum and dad have a beautiful country property with a small lake and jetty. I have sat and looked at the jetty many times and, one day, it occurred to me: I can fit a long table on that jetty! I instantly knew this location would be perfect for my birthday lunch – and that was the only thought I needed to start planning the party!

A LAKESIDE LUNCH

 There is a beautiful peony farm near my parent's place. Peonies are my absolute favourite flowers, so walking into the peony fields and picking what I need to decorate the table is my idea of heaven. Peonies come in a variety of shapes and shades, and for my table colour theme, I selected pale pink. The peonies running along the table in classic blue and white chinoiserie-style pots atop the lettuce-green linen cloth create a bright and beautiful setting. The colour combination also looks amazing against the backdrop of the lake, and reflects the tranquility of the water.

I used blue-and-white printed china plates and side plates, sitting them opposite bright-green wine glasses and patterned green napkins to anchor the look. Blue-and-white placemats add interest and complement my plates. This combination of colours works so well with the delicate flowers.

When my guests arrive, they will be welcomed in a drinks area with a beautiful grazing table adjourning to the jetty. The grazing table forms the informal first course; everyone can greet each other and chat before sitting down at the table for the main meal. Breaking the meal up like this makes it feel more casual. Setting the lunch up in this way also takes advantage of the stunning countryside, which acts as an extension of my lunch table decorations.

Grazing tables have become very popular, and creating the perfect table setting that reflects your theme is enjoyable. It does take a little bit of fiddling with, but, if you are organised and have all your props ready to go, you will find it falls into place.

As my grazing table acts as the entrée, I want to serve a variety of things, from different cheeses, breads and dips to ham, salami, grapes, fresh pears and figs – the list goes on. Grazing tables are all about abundance, so think about creating layers to display your food, with chopping boards, cake stands, books, a variety of different-sized bowls – anything to create height across your spread. Set your plates up first, then start to spread your food around, place your meat selection on the boards with cheese to match, keeping cutlery always in reach. Fill in the gaps with bunches of grapes, collections of nuts, fresh figs and herbs.

SUMMER DIPS

 Dips are simple, delicious and, with minimal effort, can look great styled up on a platter or grazing table. As always, the best dips are those homemade from fresh and flavoursome ingredients.

But, dips aren't just for dipping. Sure, there is nothing better than sitting down with wine and a platter of cheese and dips, but have you thought about using dips in your everyday cooking? How about sandwiches with dip spread on them instead of mayo or butter? Or homemade souvlakis topped with a fresh and zingy tzatziki? Don't be afraid to skip dressings either, and incorporate dips into your salads; it will give a textural element that will lift a basic salad.

TOP TIPS FOR GRAZING TABLES

◈ Create height using different platters and stands to give your table dimension. Start from the back and work from highest to lowest – a flat table is a no-no.

◈ If possible, stick to just a few colours for your boards and platters. The colour will come mainly from the food. Once it is all set up, step back and see where you can balance out the colour by swapping ingredients around.

◈ Don't worry if you don't have a tremendous amount of crockery to fill the table; chopping boards can be found in many cheap homeware stores, and having a variety of sizes will do the trick. Don't be scared to place food directly on your table either (you can even run a sheet of brown butcher's paper under everything).

◈ Use props to make your table look fuller. Set up your food around potted plants, piles of books or even groups of candles. Items that will give you height and add a little interest are what you are looking for.

◈ Include your drinks station on the table to create a more abundant, decadent look. A few bottles of bubbles in ice-filled buckets with glasses at the ready, or a few varieties of gin surrounded by cut lemons, limes and cucumbers next to an array of tumblers turns your grazing table into a banquet.

SUN-DRIED TOMATO AND GOAT'S CHEESE DIP

140 g (5 oz) julienne-cut sun-dried tomatoes, oil drained, plus extra chopped sun-dried tomatoes to garnish

3 tablespoons extra-virgin olive oil

1 teaspoon dried oregano

1 rosemary sprig, leaves stripped and chopped, plus an extra sprig to garnish

125 g (4½ oz/½ cup) low-fat sour cream

140 g (5 oz) goat's cheese, plus extra to garnish if desired

–

MAKES: 350 G (12½ OZ)
TIME: 20 MINUTES

In a food processor, combine the sun-dried tomatoes, olive oil, oregano and rosemary with a pinch of salt and pepper. Pulse until chunky.

Add the sour cream and goat's cheese, then blend for approximately 5–6 minutes until smooth. If the dip still seems a little thick, add another splash of olive oil.

Serve chilled or at room temperature. When ready to serve, crumble over some extra goat's cheese, chopped sun-dried tomatoes and another drizzle of olive oil. Garnish with a rosemary sprig.

This dip can be stored in an airtight container in the refrigerator for up to 4 days. It is best served with crackers or flatbread.

SPINACH AND WATER CHESTNUT DIP

185 g (6½ oz/¾ cup) Greek-style yoghurt

185 g (6½ oz/¾ cup) sour cream

185 g (6½ oz/¾ cup) mayonnaise

1½ teaspoons onion powder

1 teaspoon paprika

¼ teaspoon garlic powder

1½ teaspoons salt

¾ teaspoon ground black pepper

460 g (1 lb) frozen spinach, thawed and chopped

60 g (2 oz/½ cup) chopped spring onions (scallions)

1 × 225 g (8 oz) tin water chestnuts, drained and finely chopped

2 teaspoons Worcestershire sauce

–

MAKES: 1 KG (2 LB 3 OZ)
TIME: 15 MINUTES

In a large bowl, combine the yoghurt, sour cream, mayonnaise, onion powder, paprika, garlic powder, salt and pepper. Mix well.

Squeeze the spinach over the sink to get rid of any excess liquid. Add the spinach to the bowl along with the spring onion, water chestnuts and Worcestershire sauce.

Mix everything together well, then cover and refrigerate for at least 1 hour before serving. The dip can be stored in an airtight container in the refrigerator for up to 4 days. It is best served with crisp, hard crackers or lavosh.

SALMON ROE TARAMASALATA

100 g (3½ oz) crustless white bread, coarsely torn

100 g (3½ oz) salmon roe, plus extra to serve

1 small, golden shallot, finely chopped

½ small garlic clove, finely chopped

125 ml (4 fl oz/½ cup) extra-virgin olive oil

125 ml (4 fl oz/½ cup) vegetable oil

2–3 tablespoons lemon juice

–

MAKES: 350 G (12½ OZ)
TIME: 20 MINUTES, PLUS RESTING

Place the bread in a bowl and cover it with cold water, then immediately tip out the water and squeeze any excess water out of the bread.

Transfer the soggy bread to a food processor, then add the roe, shallot and garlic and process to a smooth paste. With the motor running, gradually add the oils until the mixture is thick and emulsified, then add the lemon juice to taste and season with salt and freshly ground black pepper. Make sure you try the dip before adding too much salt though – the roe is quite salty.

Cover and refrigerate overnight or for up to 3 days to allow the flavours to develop. This dip is best served with soft or crisp flatbread.

A GIN-INSPIRED BAR FOR THE LADIES

HOW TO MAKE THE PERFECT G&T

◈ The key to a great gin and tonic is to balance the bitterness of the tonic water against the gin.

◈ The flavour of the gin will also dictate the garnish used: will it need lemon, lime or cucumber? Perhaps a sprig of rosemary? There are many flavoured gins available now, so a little taste-testing may be required when perfecting your tipple. Sometimes you will need to adjust recipes depending on how you take your gin, but this is something to play with and is all part of the fun! Glassware is also something not set in stone. A great cut-glass tumbler is traditional, but I have had some beautiful gin cocktails in wine and Champagne glasses and they tasted just as sweet.

◈ Add a handful of ice to a highball glass. Pour over your gin and give it a swirl. Add your tonic to fill your glass about halfway, then finish with your garnish of choice.

Tip
If you don't like your gin watered down with ice cubes, how about making ice cubes out of tonic water? Add a garnish of fresh herbs, edible flowers or citrus to the cubes for a gorgeous added detail.

A brilliant gin bar could never be a bad thing. Using a variety of boutique and local gins, I have created a space to concoct a few blends. Using a beautiful tray laden with all the garnishes a gin could possibly need helps to make it all the more exciting and inviting. To create your own bar setting, you will need …

A variety of gins

A variety of tonics

An abundance of ice

Freshly sliced lemons and limes

Basil, thyme, mint and rosemary sprigs

Long slices of short (Lebanese) cucumbers

Star anise

Burnt orange rind, pre-curled

Different-sized glasses

A PEONY GIFT

My guests never leave empty-handed. It's a habit that I have happily fallen into and don't plan on changing anytime soon. My birthday is no different, and for this occasion, I have bundled up a posy from the local peony farm with a matching ribbon for each of my girlfriends to take home as a beautiful reminder of a gorgeous day.

Peonies are my favourite blooms, so taking good care of them and extending their life is something I spend a lot of time doing.

I love being able to watch peonies slowly expand from tight little buds into immense and intricate blooms. If they are fresh and locally grown, not frozen or imported, they can last 5–8 days as they enter full bloom.

HOW TO KEEP YOUR PEONIES HAPPY

◈ Peonies love to have their water changed regularly; about every 3 days is good.

◈ Only buy peonies that are grown locally and, if they have not been 'conditioned', make sure you do this before you put them in a vase. Conditioning peonies involves removing all the leaves.

◈ Cut all peony stems at an angle so they can easily draw water. A trick is to sit them in hot water to encourage them to bloom, but not for too long.

ETIQUETTE

◈ A lunch with the ladies really inspires the old-fashioned in me. I love the formality associated with events: the invite, the dress codes and the RSVP. These things all take that little extra time, but make such a difference in the organisation of the day.

◈ RSVP etiquette depends on the type of invitation, but it can never be done fast enough. Get it out of the way before you forget! If you received a formal invitation, then a formal RSVP should be sent via card or small note. If the invitation has an email RSVP, then you can go ahead and RSVP electronically.

◈ A hostess gift is a must. If someone has taken the time to entertain you as their guest, return the compliment by bringing a small gift. It doesn't have to be extravagant – a simple posy or a nice bottle of sparkling wine will suffice. It shows you care and appreciate being hosted.

◈ Thank you letters are a joy to receive and even more of a joy to send. It shows our friends and family that we are grateful for being hosted, that we enjoyed ourselves and that we are willing to go out of our way to let them know. It's a lovely gesture and you will be remembered for it – guaranteed. A simple letter should state your host's name(s), a thank you with a specific sentiment (thank you for the lovely roast chicken/blue cardigan/tickets to the opera) and a note to say that you look forward to seeing them again, then end with your regards. Simple.

CHINESE NEW YEAR

DRAGONS AND FIRECRACKERS

66 As a girl growing up in suburban Melbourne, Australia, every Sunday night was special; we always had delicious Chinese for dinner.

It was a family tradition that continued until my children were born, and I have some very fond memories of those days. When we were younger, Chinese food seemed exotic – the surprises inside dumplings, that first bite of Peking duck, and the fun of using chopsticks. Ever since, I have had a soft spot for Chinese food.

Chinese New Year is such a great festival to enjoy and participate in. I'm sure that most of us have seen a Chinese lion or dragon dancing through the streets come festival time, or been shocked by the wonderful noise of firecrackers going off. And, if you are at all like me, you have enjoyed and left these festivals wanting to know more about their fantastical events, which are steeped in tradition.

CELEBRATING

" There is no one way to celebrate Chinese New Year. Different parts of China have varying traditions, so get creative with your occasion and make it your own. Here are five of the most common Chinese New Year traditions.

NEW YEAR'S EVE DINNER

" The New Year's Eve dinner is the most important dinner of the year in Chinese culture. It's a time where the whole family comes together, bringing relatives from near and far to celebrate. This dinner is usually held at home and typically includes fish and dumplings, which signify prosperity.

CLEANING

Now, this tradition feels familiar to me … although it's more of a year-round thing. In the lead-up to Chinese New Year, people will do a complete clean of their house and homewares, which is all about removing the old and welcoming the new. I love the sentiment behind this practice.

RED PACKETS

You'll see lots of red packets or envelopes during Chinese New Year. Red packets containing money are gifted to children by their adult relatives during New Year's visits. It is believed that this simple gesture and sentiment conveys hope for a year of good fortune and blessings. I love seeing the little collections of red packets in Asian grocery stores. They look so inviting, and I am always trying to think of ways to use them in my styling.

FIREWORKS

I love fireworks! And I love that in Chinese tradition, fireworks are used for driving away evil. So, as the clocks strike twelve, let that cracker go. And, if you are the first to do so, you will have a year full of good luck.

DECORATION

Of course, after cleaning comes the decorating to welcome in the New Year, and it involves a lot of red – a lucky colour for the Chinese. Popular Chinese New Year decorations include lanterns, kumquats and mandarins, fresh flowers (such as peonies and plum blossom), paper decorations featuring auspicious Chinese words (especially *fu*, fortune, written in Chinese calligraphy) and posters of Chinese deities.

THE
TABLE

 What I love about creating a Chinese New Year celebration is the vivid use of red, the lush satin fabrics and the theatrics that go hand-in-hand with the event. So, when I started planning my dinner, I wanted to focus on these elements, and they ended up forming the foundation of what would be quite a regal celebration.

I love finding exciting and fun places to have an event, and an antiques store was a great location to create this Chinese New Year table setting. I fell in love with the idea of creating an all-red dining space among amazing old pieces of furniture and curios. The incredible pop of colour against the quieter backdrop is dramatic and opulent and gives a little edge to the Chinese tradition. Now, of course we aren't all able to host Chinese New Year celebrations in an antiques store, but coming up with a unique dining space is on your mind now, isn't it? Let's get creative.

The table setting is the feature of the night, and red silk cloth is the perfect starting point for the luxurious theme we are working with. Add a little extra glamour with pops of gold by using all-gold cutlery and chopsticks. Finally, finish off your table with bright-red wine and water glasses.

The centre of the table is where all the drama lives, with red ginger jars in varying shapes and sizes. If that isn't looking luxurious enough, add the final touch: lush red satin napkins. These are easily made if you have some basic sewing skills and they sit perfectly alongside gold plates and luxurious-looking gold chopsticks. Talk about glamour!

WHO SITS WHERE?

I found these gorgeous glass kumquats to attach name cards to for place settings. Have some fun choosing a font that matches the occasion to tie the look together. There are so many out there you can use, but be selective and go for something ornate that matches the feel of the event. The glass kumquats are also perfect keepsakes, as guests can take them home in a beautiful red box tied with ribbon.

DIY FORTUNE COOKIES

These are a really simple yet fun place setting. It's also a great conversation starter, as you can tailor your fortunes to match your guests.

origami or coloured craft paper (small sheets of origami paper make one fortune cookie per sheet)

drinking glass

pencil

scissors

white paper (for the fortune messages)

craft or PVA glue, or hot glue gun

paper clips (optional)

–

Turn your origami paper to the non-printed side, then place the glass on top and trace around the edge to create a circle. Repeat to make as many cookies as you would like, then cut out the circles.

Write your special messages on the white paper, then cut it into smaller strips that you can tuck inside the cookies.

To shape the cookies, place your message in the centre of a paper circle. Loosely fold the top of the circle down into the centre, parallel to the message paper strip, ensuring not to flatten down the crease line. Next, fold the bottom of the circle up into the centre. Gently create a light crease in the centre, perpendicular to the direction of the folds. Next, hold the folded circle between the thumb and index finger of one hand, with the long edge in a vertical position. Then, using the thumb and index finger of your other hand, bring the short edges of the paper together over the non-folded side of the circle to create the fortune cookie shape. Secure the cookie in place by fixating it with glue on the inside of the crease. (Tip: Use a paperclip to hold everything in position while the glue dries.)

COLOUR! COLOUR! COLOUR!

In traditional Chinese art and culture, colour plays a very important role. Black, red, green, white and yellow are viewed as colours that correspond to the five elements of water, fire, wood, metal and earth.

◈ Black corresponds to water and is regarded as a neutral colour. In modern China, black is a feature of everyday wear.

◈ Red corresponds to fire and symbolises good fortune and joy. It is heavily used during Chinese New Year and other celebrations, as well as by the government.

◈ Green is linked to health, prosperity and harmony. China's most popular gem, jade, is also a beautiful shade of green.

◈ White corresponds to metal and symbolises brightness, purity and fulfillment. White is also associated with death and mourning. Historically, the people of ancient China only wore white clothing and hats when they mourned for the dead.

◈ Yellow corresponds to earth. In China, it is considered the most beautiful and prestigious colour and is associated with heroism. It often replaces gold, is typically paired with red, and is frequently used to decorate royal palaces, altars and temples.

HAPPY DRAGON COCKTAIL

ice cubes

30–45 ml (1–1½ fl oz) ginger-infused vodka

juice of 2 tangerines

splash of lychee syrup (use the syrup from a tin of lychees)

ginger ale, to serve

skewered lychee, to garnish

–

SERVES: 1

Fill a 235 ml (8 fl oz) Champagne flute with ice.

In a tall glass, mix the vodka, tangerine juice and lychee syrup, then strain into the Champagne flute.

Top with ginger ale and garnish with a lychee on a skewer.

TIP

To make your own ginger-infused vodka, cut your desired amount of ginger into slices and place it in a clean container. Pour the vodka over the ginger and leave to infuse for 3–7 days, shaking regularly. Strain the vodka through a sieve and use it in your cocktail creations.

I love the idea of adding a swizzle stick to garnish your cocktail. I found a happy dragon at our local $2 shop. It is a collection of gold coins hanging off a red satin cord. You can attach this to a chopstick to make your very own swizzle stick – so easy!

SAN CHOI BOW

1 teaspoon sesame oil

2 tablespoons soy sauce

2 tablespoons oyster sauce

1 tablespoon peanut oil

500 g (1 lb 2 oz) minced (ground) chicken

3 shallots, thinly sliced

1 teaspoon finely grated ginger

2 garlic cloves, crushed

4 button mushrooms, finely chopped

1 × 220 g (8 oz) tin bamboo shoots, drained, finely chopped

1 × 220 g (8 oz) tin water chestnuts, drained, finely chopped

30 g (1 oz/½ cup) fried noodles

10 small iceberg lettuce leaves, washed, dried and trimmed

1 tablespoon sesame seeds, to garnish

2 tablespoons crushed peanuts, to garnish

–

MAKES: 10
TIME: 30 MINUTES

Combine the sesame oil, soy and oyster sauces in a small jug or bowl.

Heat a wok over a high heat until smoking hot, then add the peanut oil and chicken mince. Stir-fry for 3–4 minutes until it is just cooked through, breaking up the mince as you go.

Add two-thirds of the shallots, the ginger, garlic, mushrooms, bamboo shoots and chestnuts to the mince. Stir-fry for 2 minutes.

Add the combined sesame oil sauce, stirring until the mixture is heated through and the sauce has thickened slightly, then stir in the noodles.

Divide the mince mixture evenly between the lettuce cups and top with sesame seeds, nuts and the remaining shallots.

UNDERSTANDING CHINESE NEW YEAR MOTIFS

Firecrackers are heard popping throughout Chinese New Year. Their noise wards off evil spirits, and they are often lit in front of stores and homes. Wrapped in shiny paper (usually red and gold for good luck and wealth), these crackers are also used as decorations in homes, on tables and hanging on doors. Crackers are used before the New Year's Eve dinner as a sort of welcome to the celebration. They are also used at the stroke of midnight to celebrate the coming of the new year.

The colour red is one of the luckiest colours in Chinese tradition, standing for loyalty, success and happiness. We see it in the use of red packets containing monetary gifts that are handed out among families, in the packaging of firecrackers and on the dancing lions and dragons.

Kumquats are gorgeous to have around your home during the two-week period of Chinese New Year. The colour orange is a symbol of abundance, happiness and prosperity, and sharing orange fruits, such as kumquats and mandarins, with your relatives is seen as a mark of respect to your family and tradition. Golden-hued fruits are displayed everywhere, from offices to shops and cars. It is also customary to display them in your home, often next to the front door, as they are said to double your chances of wealth and prosperity.

In Chinese culture, dragons are nothing like the dragons I grew up with in fairytales. They do not swoop in and kidnap, fight or even eat poor young maidens. Instead, they represent good luck, wealth and wisdom, and are a symbol of power. They are said to have control of water, rainfall, typhoons and floods, and the colours on their bodies often represent these natural elements. They dance at Chinese New Year celebrations to ward off evil and, the longer they are, the luckier they are – some are up to 100 metres (328 feet) long!

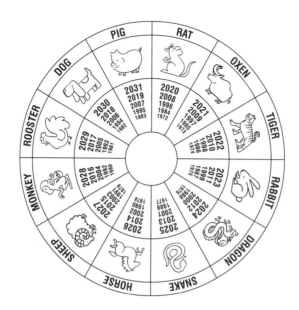

VALENTINE'S DAY

ALL YOU
NEED IS LOVE

> 66 It will come as no surprise that I am a total romantic. Valentine's Day is a day that I love and will always celebrate. It doesn't just have to be a romantic day for you and your partner; it can be a day to celebrate everyone in your life that you love. Friends, family, neighbours – it can be shared with one and all.

Valentine's Day is believed to have started off as something very different, back in the pre-Roman Empire days. It originally involved a ritual of skinning animals and running about naked, slapping people with the hides. It was believed that this practice increased fertility and drove away evil spirits. It doesn't sound like too much fun, does it?

Thankfully, Valentine's Day has since evolved into a day for celebrating love in all its forms. Since the early twentieth century, we have been gifting and passing cards to each other with a twinkle in our eyes. I love a romantic dinner for two: a gorgeous table set with beautiful glassware and china, and a delicious menu to match. The care and thought that goes into creating such a setting is, to me, the perfect gift and a beautiful act of love. Keep in mind, though, that Valentine's Day isn't all about pretty gifts. Spending time with your loved ones, cooking their favourite meal and settling in for a movie is an equal expression of love and appreciation.

A SPECIAL VALENTINE'S DAY DINNER

 I love the idea of creating a wonderful dinner for my husband on this very romantic night. Something unique, creative and memorable, and maybe a little extravagant – something I know he will love. Now, this may sound a little over the top and crazy, but a Valentine's Day dinner set-up in a little cobblestone laneway with a fabulous street art–covered wall as the backdrop was my plan. Too much, I hear you say? Oh well, too late! Now, I know this isn't possible for everyone to do, but I want to inspire you to open your mind and look beyond the dining room for other places for settings.

I found a very cute tuk-tuk for hire that I set up as a kitchen to prepare our dinner. I used the front section as a bar, where I served my romantic Valentine's Day cocktail from. The colour theme for this celebration was pink and red. As with all events, if you start introducing too many colours, you lose impact, so try to keep the setting bold.

Don't just focus on the table; the walls that surround you can also be a canvas to get creative with. To set the scene in the laneway, you could decorate the feature wall with a romantic piece of art, but a simple set of initials in a love heart or an intimate message to your partner drawn with chalk would also lend a casual, personal feel to the evening.

If you're setting a table for two, it must be completed with a dramatic cloth. You can buy fabric by the metre from your local fabric store, which is such an inexpensive way to dress a table. Buy enough so that your tablecloth drapes in abundance, upping the drama.

My collection of pink and red glassware and china suits this setting perfectly, and no Valentine's dinner would be complete without the inclusion of flowers. The rose is a classic symbol of Valentine's Day, and I love using specimen vases to create a heart shape on the table. It's just a little way to mix it up rather than having a normal bunch of roses, and it makes your bunch go a lot further.

VALENTINE'S DAY MENU

My idea of a heavenly Valentine's Day meal involves shrimp, a light meringue for dessert and a delicious cocktail. The shrimp cocktail was brought to fame by an English TV chef in the 1960s and, after many rebirths and reinventions, I am not ashamed to say that there is nothing nicer than the crunch of iceberg lettuce with a drenched shrimp. Easy to make and light to eat, a shrimp cocktail is the perfect first act of a Valentine's Day menu. Followed by a gorgeously pink Eton Mess and a cocktail, what more could you want?

MARKET-FRESH PEELED SHRIMP AND HOMEMADE MAYO

2 free-range egg yolks

1 heaped teaspoon dijon mustard

500 ml (17 fl oz/2 cups) olive oil

1–2 tablespoons white-wine vinegar

pinch of sea salt

½ lemon

250 g (9 oz) market-fresh cooked peeled shrimp

–

SERVES: 2
TIME: 15 MINUTES

Whisk the egg yolks in a bowl, then add the mustard and whisk until well combined. Gradually add about half the oil, very slowly at first, whisking continuously for around 3–5 minutes, or until thickened. Next, whisk in 1 tablespoon of the vinegar. This will loosen the mixture slightly and give it a pale colour.

Gradually add the remaining oil, whisking continuously. Season with a pinch of salt, a squeeze of lemon juice and a little more vinegar, if needed.

Place the shrimp on a platter or in a bowl (on ice, if desired) and serve with the homemade mayo. Store any leftover mayo in a sterilised glass jar in the fridge for up to 1 week.

NOTE
To sterilise jars, wash them (including the lids) in a dishwasher on a slow cycle, then allow to air dry on a clean tea towel (dish towel). Alternatively, preheat the oven to 120°C (250°F). Wash the jars and lids in hot, soapy water, then place on a baking tray and transfer to the oven for 20 minutes to fully dry out.

Iceberg lettuce with yoghurt dressing

SERVES: 2
TIME: 10 MINUTES

30 g (1 oz) thick, Greek-style yoghurt

juice of ¼ lemon

⅛ preserved lemon, flesh and white pith discarded, rind finely chopped

½ tablespoon finely chopped thyme leaves

1 tablespoon extra-virgin olive oil

½ small iceberg lettuce, cored, quartered

5 g (¼ oz) mint leaves

½ Lebanese (short) cucumber, cut into 1 cm (½ in) pieces

100 g (3½ oz) feta, crumbled

–

To make the dressing, combine the yoghurt, lemon juice, preserved lemon, thyme leaves and half the olive oil in a bowl. Season well with salt and pepper.

Place a wedge of lettuce on each plate, scatter with mint leaves and chopped cucumber, then drizzle with the dressing. Crumble the feta over the top, then drizzle with the remaining olive oil. Season to taste, then serve. Alternatively, arrange all ingredients in a large glass bowl to share and serve alongside the shrimp and mayo.

A WORD ON SHRIMP

I love to cook with shrimp. They are simple, versatile and packed with flavour. Although many fresh-food markets sell frozen raw shrimp to preserve their flavour and texture straight off the boat, it's worth seeking out fresh ones. Whether buying fresh or frozen, look for shrimp with their heads attached and those with tight, firm shells that have a sheen to them. Leave your shrimp in their shells until they are ready to be cooked (up to a maximum of 3 days in the fridge or 3 months in the freezer). Like most seafood, shrimp cook quickly.

ETON MESS

Eton Mess is a dreamy dessert for Valentine's Day; it's simple to pull together and is always delicious. Bringing out all components and building it at the table with your loved one is a lot of fun. My tip is to add chocolate to the traditional Eton Mess mixture. My personal favourite is flaked almond milk chocolate, as it just adds another textural crunch.

375 g (13 oz) strawberries, hulled and quartered, plus extra to serve

60 g (2 oz/¼ cup) caster (superfine) sugar

100 ml (3½ fl oz) thickened (whipping) cream, lightly whisked

60 ml (2 fl oz/¼ cup) crème fraîche

30 g (1 oz/¼ cup) icing (confectioners') sugar, sifted

¼ vanilla bean, split lengthways and seeds scraped

50 g (1¾ oz) chocolate of your choice, roughly broken (thinner blocks are best, or roughly chop a thicker block)

60 g (2 oz/½ cup) raspberries, to serve

mint leaves, to serve

Meringue

2 egg whites

pinch of salt

50 g (1¾ oz) caster (superfine) sugar

50 g (1¾ oz) icing (confectioners') sugar, sifted

8 g (¼ oz) cornflour (cornstarch)

–

SERVES: 2
TIME: 1 HOUR

Preheat the oven to 120°C (250°F). Line two baking trays with baking paper.

To make the meringue, whisk the egg whites with a pinch of salt using an electric mixer (or free-standing electric mixer) until firm peaks form, about 3–4 minutes. With the motor still running, gradually add the caster sugar and whisk for another 2–3 minutes until thick and glossy. Sift the icing sugar and cornflour over the mixture, then gently fold in.

Spoon 8 cm (3¼ in) mounds of the meringue, spaced well apart, onto the prepared trays. Bake for 40–50 minutes until the meringues lift easily from the baking paper and are crisp but not coloured, then turn off the oven and leave the meringues inside, with the door ajar, to cool completely.

Meanwhile, toss the strawberries and caster sugar in a large bowl, then set aside for about 20 minutes until the juices begin to seep out of the strawberries.

Whisk the cream, crème fraîche, icing sugar and vanilla seeds together in a separate large bowl until soft peaks form. Set aside.

Scatter one-quarter of the strawberries in the base of two serving dishes (glasses or bowls work equally well). Spread with one-quarter of the cream mixture and coarsely crumble one-quarter of the meringue and broken chocolate over the top. Continue layering with the remaining ingredients.

Scatter the Eton Mess with raspberries and extra strawberries, if desired, to serve, and garnish with fresh mint and chunks of chocolate.

VALENTINE'S COCKTAIL

A table setting this romantic needs a special cocktail to match. A beautiful aperitif to start a meal is always a treat, and this is the perfect night for it. All you need to do is hand it to your special someone as you lead them towards the table and let the night of romance begin.

45 ml (1½ fl oz) dry gin or vodka

125 ml (4 fl oz/½ cup) freshly squeezed pink grapefruit juice

30 ml (1 fl oz) Rosemary syrup (see below)

ice cubes, for shaking and serving

1 fresh rosemary sprig and 1 pink grapefruit slice, to garnish

Rosemary syrup (*see Note*)

115 g (4 oz/½ cup) caster (superfine) sugar

2 rosemary sprigs, leaves stripped and stalks discarded

–

SERVES: 1

For the rosemary syrup, combine the sugar and rosemary sprigs with 125 ml (4 fl oz/½ cup) water in a small saucepan. Stir to combine, then bring to the boil. Reduce the heat, cover with a lid and simmer for 3 minutes. Turn off the heat and let the mixture steep for another 5 minutes before straining through a fine-mesh sieve. Discard the rosemary and allow the syrup to cool before transferring to a sterilised bottle or jar (see page 50). The syrup will keep for a couple of weeks in an airtight jar, stored in a cool, dark place.

Combine the gin, grapefruit juice and rosemary syrup in a shaker. Add a big scoop of ice and shake vigorously for 20 seconds, or until the shaker feels icy cold in your hands.

Fill a highball glass with ice and strain the cocktail through a strainer or fine-mesh sieve into the glass.

Garnish with fresh rosemary and a grapefruit slice.

NOTE
This syrup is also delicious when used in a lemon and ginger margarita.

VALENTINE'S DAY DIY GIFTING

 A handmade gift is just as meaningful as a store-bought one, if not more so because of the sentiment behind it. This is especially so on Valentine's Day, where a heartfelt, handmade present is perfect. So, let's make that special someone a unique gift that comes just from you, a gift that celebrates your life and times together and memories that you have made: a memory jar.

FILL YOUR MEMORY JAR WITH COLLECTIONS FROM YOUR PAST. HERE ARE SOME IDEAS:

- Photos
- Letters
- Movie tickets of a particular date
- Decorations with each of your initials on them
- Love trinkets, like hearts, cupid decorations ...
- Jewellery
- Feathers
- Buttons from a favourite shirt
- An old tape
- Lace from your wedding dress
- Airline tickets
- Small bottle of perfume
- Hanky
- Dried flowers
- Baby's lock of hair
- Cufflinks
- Reel of cotton (1st wedding anniversary)
- A handwritten love poem or significant song lyrics

SYMBOLISM OF THE HEART

❖ The heart has been used as a symbol of love since the thirteenth century. Some say this was due to the artists of the Middle Ages, who used heart-shaped leaves in their paintings to represent romantic love, as well as the love between humanity and God.

❖ Devout Christians began incorporating the iconic symbol in their art and literature as a representation of Jesus Christ and his love and, when Valentine's Day became increasingly associated with romantic love in the Middle Ages, the heart became synonymous with this special holiday.

ROMANTIC MOVIE LIST

Sometimes, the simplest things are the best, and a movie night is just that. I love snuggling up on the couch, having a glass of wine and some snacks and watching a romantic movie with a loved one.

❖ *Chocolat*

❖ *An Affair to Remember*

❖ *Love Actually*

❖ *Ghost*

❖ *Doctor Zhivago*

❖ *Notting Hill*

❖ *The English Patient*

❖ *Titanic*

❖ *The Bridges of Madison County*

❖ *The Notebook*

❖ *Before Sunset – the trilogy*

❖ *The Fault in Our Stars*

❖ *Roman Holiday*

❖ *Me Before You*

HOW TO WRITE THE PERFECT LOVE LETTER

A love letter may seem like a simple Valentine's Day gift, but, once you sit down to write, you might find that it's a little trickier than you'd imagined. All of a sudden, there is so much to say, and if you are not practiced at writing, it may seem a little daunting. But, take a breath, take your time and write from the heart.

- How do you want your recipient to feel? Focus on this as you write down the reasons why you love them.

- Give details about why you love them, give examples and make it reflect your life together. Talk about the great times you have had and the beautiful memories you have made.

- It's the small things that our partners do that keep relationships humming along smoothly. Mention these small things; things that you love about them; things they do to make you feel special.

- Write in your own voice. Just because it's a love letter doesn't mean that it has to be flowery and full of grand declarations. Keep it simple and keep it real.

- Tell them how they make you feel, confirm your love and share it.

A BOX FOR YOUR SWEETHEART

◈ **Date night:** Fill a heart-shaped box with movie tickets, candy bar vouchers and an assortment of candy. Anything that will keep both of you smiling on date night.

◈ **For the sweet tooth:** A heart-shaped box traditionally comes ready-filled with delicious boutique chocolates, but how about making your own? If you're short on time, hit the supermarket to snap up your partner's favourites and load up the box, but it will feel all the more heartfelt if you've had a go at making them yourself. You can find cute chocolate moulds in a myriad of shapes online to fill with melted chocolate. Try to find a shape that is meaningful to both of you. This is the perfect gift to give just after an intimate dinner – dessert is served!

◈ **Love letter kit:** Ever dreamt of receiving the most perfectly written love letter? Whether it's from an anonymous admirer or your life partner, reading words of love is one of the most heartwarming feelings in the world, especially when they have been written on something that can be treasured forever. So, why not make a little writing kit as a gift? Fill your box with note paper and envelopes, a lovely pen, a few prompts to get them started and, of course, a letter from you to your beloved.

EASTER

DECORATE WITH FLOWERS

66 There is nothing I love more than the celebrations over Easter. They come at such a perfect time, with winter behind us and warmer days starting to rear their heads, offering you the chance to get away and catch up with family and friends.

Easter is also a fun time to decorate your home with beautiful flowers and plants that can be enjoyed for a few days. We always host a big lunch, and having some time to prepare is absolute bliss. It also gives me a chance to play with my white crockery collection, which is growing larger every year. I look forward to Easter, not just for the chocolate, but so that I can carry on my own Easter traditions of relaxing, decorating and spending time with family, and adding to my collection of very special bunnies.

For years, I have been collecting white Easter china that I love to use when celebrating this time of year. It includes rabbit jugs and cake stands, themed bowls and plates. It's fun to have a collection that you only use once a year, as you always have to think of new, creative ways to use it. In the past, I have surrounded these items with garden cabbages and birds' nests, hidden them in climbing vines across a sideboard and layered them with sweets. This Easter, my plan is to set a whimsical table layered with my china bunnies in a field of wild daisies.

THE
TABLE

" The Easter lunch is always the highlight of the weekend, so a gorgeous lunch setting must be created. My parents' home has the most amazing field of daisies, and it just shines at Easter time, so, for my table, I decided that it had to be outdoors among the daisies.

It may seem a little crazy, but dragging the dining table outdoors really made this set-up so special. As a family, we eat together all the time, so with each occasion we celebrate I like to try to outshine the last. Making a simple change, like dining outdoors, really made this an event to remember.

For my setting I chose not to use a tablecloth but to have the wood grain of the table show through. To really maximise the visual impact, I like to layer up plates with at least two different sizes. This adds height and interest to the table and gives me an opportunity to add some colour or texture.

There are so many fabulous plates around, and I do love layering old with new. Mixing and matching is lots of fun (now you see why I have such a crazy collection of plates). You can separate plates with a napkin or stylishly drape it near each setting, adding more texture and height to the table.

A dear girlfriend once gave me a collection of beautiful blue placemats. As soon as I saw them I knew they would be perfect for Easter. The shape and contrast of the pale blue and white on the wooden table looks perfect, and including matching serviettes adds a sense of cohesion to the table.

For special occasions, you should use place settings for your guests. I see these as a finishing touch to a table, and I love to give my guests a small gift. Placing the gift in the table setting combines the two and gives the table an extra layer to bring the look together. Being Easter, giving an egg of some sort is a must, so I placed pale blue chocolate eggs on top of hand-made baby bird's nests. Adorned with sugar flowers, I knew these nests would make the perfect gifts for my guests to take home at the end of the day.

The centrepiece for a table is something I love to get creative with. For a clean, simple look, I used the simplest of wild flowers: daisies. There is such an innocent charm about these flowers; they perfectly reflect the excitement and wonder of Easter. I wanted to display them in a selection of white glass vessels but didn't have any. So, what did I do? Made my own, of course! The painted vases (page 70) create a line down the middle of the table, nestling in with my collection of white bunny jugs and containers. I'll be repainting them a few times in the future to match different table settings.

SLOW-ROAST LAMB

I love this recipe because it is so simple, and you can't really make a mistake. It's also a great recipe when entertaining – you can prepare it quickly and it's almost impossible to overcook.

2 kg (4 lb 6 oz) lamb shoulder, boned

2 tablespoons sea salt

2 garlic cloves, sliced

6 rosemary sprigs, leaves stripped and chopped

1 tablespoon black peppercorns

3 tablespoons dried oregano

100 ml (3½ fl oz) extra-virgin olive oil

100 ml (3½ fl oz) white vinegar

–

SERVES: 12
TIME: APPROX. 3½–4 HOURS

Preheat the oven to 150°C (300°F).

Combine the salt, garlic, rosemary, peppercorns and oregano in a bowl, then rub the mix all over the meat.

Place the seasoned shoulder in a large cast-iron pot, then pour over the olive oil, vinegar and 150 ml (5½ fl oz) water.

Cover with a lid and cook for 3½–4 hours, turning halfway through. If you want it super tender, you can continue cooking for another 30 minutes.

TIP
I love to spread a layer of Hummus (opposite) over the lamb, then top it with chickpeas, pomegranate seeds and watercress (optional) to serve.

Honey-glazed carrots

1 kg (2 lb 3 oz) baby or heirloom carrots

80 g (2¾ oz) butter

80 g (2¾ oz) honey

2 tablespoons lemon juice

½ bunch chopped flat-leaf (Italian) parsley,
to garnish (optional)

–

SERVES: 8
TIME: 15 MINUTES

Bring a saucepan of water to the boil. Add the carrots
with a good pinch of salt and boil for 5–6 minutes,
or until tender.

Drain, then return the carrots to the pan with the butter,
honey and lemon juice. Cook over a medium heat for
about 5 minutes until a glaze coats the carrots.

Season with salt and pepper and garnish with
the parsley, if desired.

Hummus

1 × 400 g (14 oz) tin chickpeas, drained and rinsed

1 garlic clove

60 ml (2 fl oz/¼ cup) olive oil, plus extra to serve

2 tablespoons fresh lemon juice

2 tablespoons tahini

1 teaspoon ground cumin

kosher salt

¼ teaspoon paprika, to garnish

–

MAKES: 350 G (12½ OZ/1½ CUPS)
TIME: 5 MINUTES

Combine all ingredients, except the paprika, in a
food processor and blitz to a smooth purée. Add
1–2 tablespoons water as necessary to achieve a
smooth and creamy consistency.

Transfer to a serving bowl, drizzle with extra olive oil
and sprinkle with the paprika.

WHY DO WE GIVE EASTER EGGS?

Brightly painted and foil-covered eggs have become part and parcel of Easter, whether they are filled with chocolate or are merely decorative. For Christians, the Easter egg symbolises the resurrection of Jesus Christ; for Orthodox and Eastern Catholic Churches, red-dyed eggs represent the blood that Jesus Christ shed on the cross.

Easter eggs are a symbol of new life and rebirth, and were traditionally hand-painted and given as gifts. By the mid-nineteenth century, John Cadbury had begun experimenting with chocolate eggs, but only perfected them in the 1870s using a pour-in chocolate mould method. The earliest chocolate Easter eggs were made with dark chocolate, but a swap to milk chocolate saw a boom in their popularity and, when mass-produced hand-painted eggs became too laborious to make, foil-wrapped versions of Easter eggs took their place.

HOW TO PAINT VASES

Use a spray paint designed for glass. Make sure you read the instructions well before choosing your paint. There really is nothing worse than knowing your idea didn't work because you forgot to read the label.

- Wash your vases thoroughly and let them dry completely before painting.
- Wipe down your vases with rubbing alcohol, then let them dry.
- Following the instructions on the tin of spray paint, start by spraying a practice spray on some newspaper as a test. You want a fresh spray of paint with no splotches.
- Hold the spray tin 20–30 cm (8–12 in) away from the vase and spray in a sweeping horizontal motion. Make sure you are spraying in a well-ventilated area and working slowly – don't rush it.
- Admire your handy work and let your vases dry.

EASTER EGG HUNT

What's Easter without an egg hunt? Regardless of age, it is so much fun to hide eggs and watch friends and family go off looking for them. Setting up a corner table ready with matching baskets, pairs of bunny ears (and a few well-placed arrows) is a must to get everyone in the spirit. Whether you are inside or outside, make sure you have a beginning and an end to your hunt and make up some fun signs to guide everyone in the right or wrong direction. You could even do this as a scavenger hunt with great Easter-themed clues and ideas along the way.

GIFTS THAT ARE NOT CHOCOLATE

Not everyone likes chocolate, and sometimes it's fun to mix up the Easter gifts. Here are some ideas:

- A beautiful bird's nest with gorgeous flowers

- Fresh farm-grown organic eggs

- A delicious carrot cake

- A box of Easter-inspired craft things, such as a colouring-in book, pencils, glue and glitter

- Gingerbread cookies beautifully decorated as eggs

- A potted plant

- Marshmallow bunny tails

- A mason jar with choc-chip cookie ingredients and a cookie cutter tied to the side

EASTER WREATH

You know me: I love any occasion to decorate the house, and Easter is one I often get carried away with. We tend to concentrate on creating a beautiful Easter table, but what about the front door? Easter wreaths are so much fun to make and are a great starting point for your overall theme.

You can find twig wreaths at most craft stores. Using this as your base, it's easy to be creative and tie your decorations on to the twigs using twine. My Easter palette this year consists of green and white with accents of pale blue. I love the idea of attaching a collection of baby birds' nests decorated with speckled coloured eggs and a little fresh moss to fill in the gaps. A beautiful blue-and-white striped grosgrain ribbon will be used to hang the wreath to the door, with extra ribbon to create the bow. I'll also leave long lengths hanging over the wreath.

MOTHER'S DAY

OH, MOTHER'S DAY

66 Oh, Mother's Day. It's that one day of the year when you get a guilt-free sleep in and then (hopefully) get to do nothing all day. I love the idea of spoiling your mum or that special woman in your life who is always there for you. It can be an aunt, your partner, your grandmother, your best friend, your best friend's mum – any woman who has been a bright, shining light in your life. It's a day to celebrate and show that special someone how much you care for and appreciate them.

A SPECIAL TREAT

As with any other occasion, it's the small gestures that often mean the most, and creating that perfect breakfast in bed is something I dream about. A tray with your favourite breakfast, a good coffee and the newspaper is the ideal start to the day, and the fact that you can dine in bed is just the icing on the cake. So, where do you begin?

Well, of course, you have to have the perfect tray. Big enough to fit all the food you want to serve, and preferably one with legs so that it can stand on the bed without the risk of anything falling off or spilling. A small flower from the garden is always a sweet touch, and using some pretty china and cutlery will also win you brownie points.

WHAT MUM WON'T TELL YOU ON MOTHER'S DAY

◈ Do not wake her up before 9 am. She needs a sleep in, and this is the one day where she gets to have it all her way.

◈ Stay quiet until she wakes up. Sure, you can start making your delicious breakfast, but do it quietly.

◈ When cooking mum's favourite breakfast, clean up as you go. Don't leave any dishes for her to do.

◈ Be prepared and have all the food you need the day before. If you can't get what's needed, then ask a family member or family friend to help.

◈ Use a tray with sides so that when you're walking in with breakfast, it doesn't fall off.

◈ After breakfast, take the tray away and let mum have a snooze or read a book or magazine.

THE PERFECT
MOTHER'S DAY
BREAKFAST

HEART-SHAPED PANCAKES WITH MIXED BERRY AND VANILLA COMPOTE

225 g (8 oz/1½ cups) plain (all-purpose) flour

2 tablespoons caster (superfine) sugar

2 teaspoons baking powder

1 teaspoon bicarbonate of soda (baking soda)

½ teaspoon salt

250 ml (8½ fl oz/1 cup) milk or buttermilk

2 large eggs

60 ml (2 fl oz/¼ cup) melted butter, plus extra for greasing

thickened (whipping) cream, to serve (optional)

Mixed berry and vanilla compote (Makes 630 g/1 lb 6 oz/2 cups)

500 g (1 lb 2 oz) frozen mixed berries

½ vanilla bean, split lengthways and seeds scraped

55 g (2 oz/¼ cup) caster (superfine) sugar

—

MAKES: 12 PANCAKES
TIME: 15 MINUTES

To make the compote, combine the berries, vanilla bean and seeds and the sugar in a saucepan over a low heat. Cook, stirring occasionally, for 8–10 minutes, or until the berries have just softened. Remove from the heat and leave to cool completely. Store any leftover compote in an airtight container in the refrigerator for up to 1 week.

In a large mixing bowl, sift together the flour, sugar, baking powder, bicarbonate of soda and salt.

Whisk in the milk, eggs and melted butter until just combined.

Preheat a flat griddle or frying pan over a medium–high heat. Grease a heart-shaped silicone egg ring with butter to prevent sticking.

Scoop 125 ml (4 fl oz/½ cup) of the pancake batter into the ring in the saucepan, or just dollop in the mixture in circles. Cook until small bubbles form on the surface of the pancake, then flip it over and cook for another 2–3 minutes on the other side.

Serve hot, with the compote on the side or piled on the pancake, and a dollop of whipped cream, if desired.

BLOOD ORANGE MIMOSA

30 ml (1 fl oz) freshly squeezed blood-orange juice

30 ml (1 fl oz) elderflower liqueur

your favourite prosecco, Champagne or other sparkling white wine of your choice, chilled

—

SERVES: 1

Combine the blood orange juice and elderflower liqueur in a Champagne flute and gently top with prosecco. Enjoy!

HOW TO MAKE THE PERFECT CUP OF TEA

Make sure you fill your kettle with fresh, oxygenated water each time. Tea loves air, and the bubbles from fresh water help the tea develop its flavour. Depending on what style of tea you are brewing, steeping times will differ. Make sure you read the packaging first, as some teas need longer and some less time to develop the best flavour.

If using a stovetop kettle, don't let your water boil over as this can burn the tea leaves. Once the water has reached boiling point, remove it from the stove immediately.

Most teas need at least 3 minutes to brew (even tea bags), so don't rush it. Once brewed, don't leave the teabag or spoon in your cup. Not only does it look bad, but it will change the flavour of the tea.

Milk never goes in your teacup first, as it's impossible to gauge how much milk will be needed to dilute the tea if you put the milk in first. Always use full-cream (whole) milk; you want to make the most of your cup of tea, so indulge a little.

THE MEANING OF FLOWERS

I love giving friends and family beautiful bunches of fresh flowers, whether it be for Mother's Day, another special occasion, or just to brighten someone's day. I always want to know the meaning of things, and flowers are no exception. Each flower variety has its own language – knowing this language makes giving a beautiful bunch that extra bit special and personal.

- Baby's breath = innocence
- Carnation = pride, love
- Chrysanthemum = optimism, joy
- Dahlia = elegance, dignity
- Daisy = innocence, cheer
- Forget-me-not = true love
- Honeysuckle = affection
- Lily of the valley = sweetness, happiness
- Orchid = beauty
- Peony = honour, prosperity, romance
- Rose (red) = true love
- Rose (white) = virtue
- Rose (yellow) = friendship
- Rose (pink) = grace
- Sunflower = adoration

HANDMADE GIFT IDEAS

I have always loved receiving handmade gifts from my kids. I still have most of them, stored away, and some in frames. There is nothing better than the look on your child's face when they watch you open a handmade gift; it is such a special moment. So, when Mother's Day comes around, encourage them to make something themselves instead of spending money on presents. Here are some ideas:

◈ Handmade tea bags (see on right)

◈ A family newspaper

◈ A cheque book–style booklet full of love notes

◈ Photobook of school-work projects

◈ Bathroom care package

◈ A homemade facial mask or a simple sugar scrub (you can find many simple recipes online)

HOMEMADE HEART TEA BAGS

I love this simple little DIY. It makes such an effective gift and really lends itself to so many themes. All you need to do is change the shape of the bag.

1 coffee filter

scissors

needle and pink sewing thread

1 tablespoon loose-leaf tea

small funnel (optional)

12.5 cm (5 in) piece of white string or thick thread

origami paper (for the tag at the end of the string)

–

MAKES: 1 TEA BAG

Flatten out a coffee filter, then cut out a heart shape. You should have two heart-shaped pieces of filter.

Sew around the edges of the heart shapes to join them, leaving a small gap that you can syphon the loose tea into.

Put the tea into the heart (you can use a small funnel to make this step easier), loop a section of string into the tea bag (this will help with dunking) and sew the opening closed.

Cut your origami paper into whatever shape you desire to make a tea bag handle.

Either hole-punch the paper and slip your string through the hole to keep it in place, or staple the paper to the thread. Done!

AN AFTERNOON OF RELAXATION

My dream Mother's Day involves a lovely, long bath. It's the perfect day to soak in some beautiful bubbly water and indulge in some 'me' time. I pour the perfect bath with clouds of bubbles, listen to a personalised music playlist, light some candles to give the bathroom a bit of mood lighting, relax and read magazines.

To guarantee that perfect relaxing afternoon and to make Mother's Day more special, put together a little 'emergency kit' for your mum, filled with a few bath bits and pieces. Fill a box with her favourite things for the ultimate day of pampering. You might like to include a new novel or magazine, a mini bottle of Champagne, a fragrant candle, luxurious bubble bath and body lotion with matching loofah, or her favourite sweet treats, so she can sip on that Champagne and indulge.

GET CREATIVE WITH GIFT GIVING

I love giving gifts, and I do put a lot of effort and thought into what I give friends and family. I love it so much that even the ritual of wrapping gets me excited. There are so many fantastic ways to wrap your gifts, it's almost an art in itself. I love to mix a little DIY into my presents, and I find that if I set an afternoon aside for organising my wrapping, cards, ribbons and tags, I am set for a whole year. Don't laugh! I have been known to spend an afternoon potato-printing brown craft paper to get the style of wrapping that I like.

◆ **Brown craft wrapping paper** A simple roll of craft paper can be the base of so many creative wrappings. Stamp it, cover it with stickers, wrap it in simple twine or garnish it with a piece of fruit – every house should have a roll of craft paper.

◆ **Furoshiki** is a Japanese wrapping cloth. It's recyclable and is a fabulous way of personalising your gifts in a way that suits your lucky recipient. By simply buying half a metre (1.6 feet) cuts of fabric from your local craft store, you can have a collection of furoshiki ready to use at a moment's notice.

◆ **Tea towel** (dish towel) When gifting food, homewares or even garden-themed gifts, I always look for cool tea towels to wrap them in. These gifts are perfect wrapped and placed in a basket. So simple and useful.

◆ **Gift boxes** A classic style of gifting that suits every occasion. A crisp box with a sharp grosgrain ribbon tied into a lush bow – what more could you want?

SUMMER
DAYS

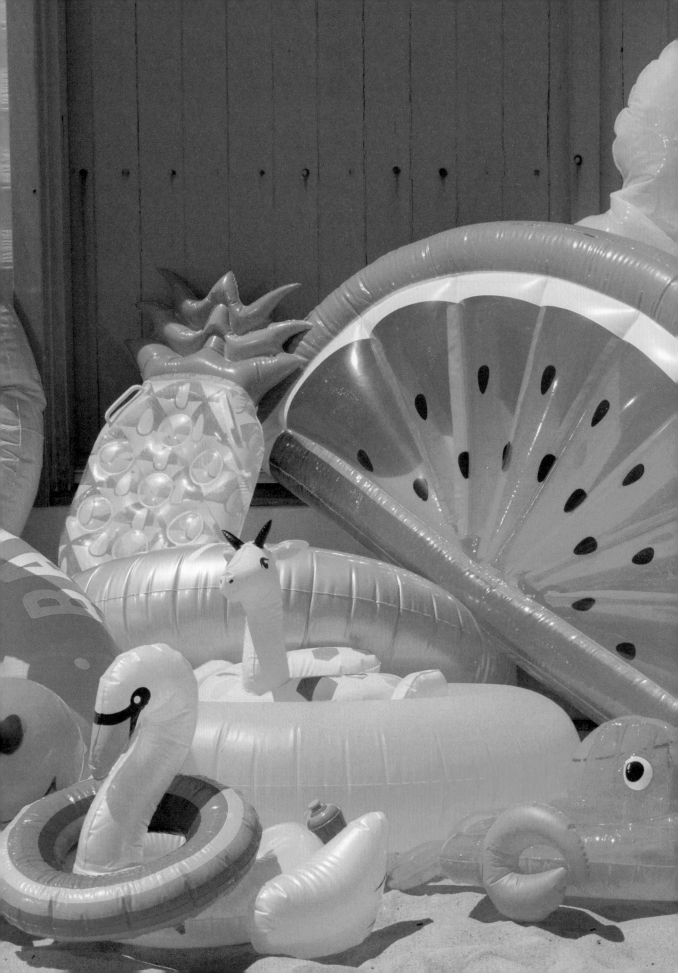

SPLISH
SPLASH!

SPLISH
SPLASH!

SUMMER LOVING

66 Hands up, who loves long, lazy, hot summer days? Being at the beach with friends and family, impromptu barbecues in the backyard, endless games of baseball or soccer on breezy, warm days – there's just something about summer that screams *party time*! And the beach is the perfect stage for these relaxed and happy gatherings.

Before we get to the party though, having a great invitation can set the tone for a fun day. With a theme as broad as summer you can go as extravagant or as casual as you like, but it does need to be bright and inviting. Why should you create an invitation to a beach party? Because everybody loves an invitation. It also formalises the event so people can plan their lives around it. Keeping it vague doesn't inspire fun, so set a time, set a place and create a day everyone will look forward to.

BEACH
BOXES

 Down on the Mornington Peninsula in south-east Victoria, Australia, there is a stretch of beach with the most beautiful coloured beach boxes. So, when I think of a beach party, my mind automatically goes to these bright, iconic beach boxes. Using them as inspiration, I wanted my beach party to be as colourful and playful as possible.

I love the idea of a European beach club and, while this may be a bit more involved to set up, it is a total hit when guests arrive. When planning your beach party, it's all about colour and using this colour en masse. A fantastic beach chair and matching towel were the starting point for my beach party décor, inspiring the pops of colour I have used for the food and drinks bar.

I think we're all familiar with the variety of blow-up beach toys, balls and mattresses available. Having as many as possible blown up and ready to use is all that's needed to get the party started. They look fantastic and are also great fun for everyone to play with or just sit and relax on.

With a beach party, it's essential to stay on top of some basic housekeeping. Everyone will arrive with lots of beach bags, so make sure you allocate a space for these. Make your bathroom signage clear for all to see. I enjoy having signs made to direct my guests. It just adds to the fun of the day, and signs are a great opportunity to personalise your décor.

Because it is summer, a fun idea is to create a suntan lotion bar near the bathrooms. It can be as simple as setting up a colourful table with a selection of lotions with different SPFs so that everyone is covered. You can add tins of spray mist, hand fans and even a collection of sunglasses and hats. Be prepared for whatever the day might bring and have a well-stocked first aid kit and insect repellent on hand too.

Now for the all-important food and drinks bar. Again, signage will help pull this look together, and you can keep it as simple as having a pair of matching tables displaying all the food and drinks. You are outdoors, so now is your chance to use disposable paper plates and cups. There are many fun designs to choose from, so stick to your theme and stock up. Surround your tables with large tin buckets full of ice with bottles of cold drinks. A beach party tradition is to have a portable chiller on hand; they're easy to transport and make great props for styling your chill-out areas.

When all is done, make sure you leave the area cleaner than you found it. Have plenty of rubbish bags (and helpers to get the job done), bring plastic wrap for leftover food, and bags for all your decorations.

SOME GREAT INVITATION IDEAS

◈ Beach balls with the invitation printed on it

◈ A pair of thongs tied with a colourful ribbon and the invitation attached

◈ A beach bat and ball. You can write the party details on the bat with permanent marker

◈ A beach hat with the request written inside the hat band

◈ A kite with the invite dangling from the string

◈ A silly pair of large sunglasses with the details written on the shades

◈ A message in a small bottle

Encourage your guests to bring novelty invitations, like beach balls and sunglasses, to the party too. They can all act as forms of entertainment, and can be used in games that kids and adults can play as the sun sets.

SANDCASTLE COMPETITION

A great bonding session for those with a competitive streak is a sandcastle competition. Have a selection of spades and buckets, and piles of seaweed, driftwood and shells that everyone can use when creating their sand masterpiece. These beachcomber items can be something that you have found before the party, or you can give guests a basket and 20 minutes to find what they need before the building commences. Set a timer and let the games begin.

SANDCASTLE BUILDING – THE BASICS

◈ Keep it simple with your building tools. You will need a shovel, funnel and, of course, a bucket. Bring some household items like a butter knife, melon baller and forks to create pattern and shapes.

◈ Use moist sand. If a ball of sand stays in your hand when squeezed, it's castle-ready.

◈ Start with building a mound and go from there. As your mound grows, pour water over it to tighten the sand.

◈ Start shaving into your mound to create your shapes; removing sand is easier than adding it.

◈ Start from the top and work your way down.

FOOD
STATIONS

" Your food station can sit next to the drinks bar and be stocked and ready to go. Keep it bright and fun with coloured paper straws and disposable paper plates. Keep all your cutlery, napkins and other utensils in buckets – they're great for matching to a theme and can be used again for making sandcastles. If you are supplying large platters of salads, how about using toy spades as serving utensils? These everyday items can be styled up in interesting ways, so get creative!

For a seaside lunch, look no further than traditional fish and chips. Talk to your local fish 'n chippery before your event and order in your meals. Depending on your number of guests, this is a much easier alternative than bringing in a deep-fryer and cooking everything yourself. To me, fish and chips have to be wrapped in newspaper. It's old-fashioned, fun and a great conversation starter. You can take this idea one step further and design and print your own paper, emblazoned with witty information about the day's activities.

After an afternoon of swimming and a lunch of delicious fish and chips, it's time to relax into sunset with a simple dessert. Frozen icy poles and ice creams or ice cream sandwiches in creative flavours are great options. Large watermelon slices cut into wedges on wooden sticks (see the image on page 104–105) are healthy alternatives for kids, and, of course, just as refreshing. For the adults, a vodka-infused watermelon gives that extra-special kick as the sun goes down (see page 105).

EASY TARTARE SAUCE

It's always important to have all the necessary condiments on hand, like mayonnaise, white vinegar, tartare sauce, ketchup, fresh lemon wedges and salt and pepper. These are simple to bring to the party pre-prepared and you can decant them into fun squeeze bottles or small dishes for easy beachside use.

200 g (7 oz) store-bought or homemade mayo (page 50)

3 tablespoons capers, drained, rinsed and chopped

3 tablespoons gherkins, drained, rinsed and chopped

1 small spring onion (scallion), finely chopped

squeeze of lemon juice

3 tablespoons chopped flat-leaf (Italian) parsley

–

SERVES: 4
TIME: 10 MINUTES

Combine all the ingredients in a small bowl and season to taste with salt and pepper. Serve straight away or refrigerate until needed.

ICEBERG LETTUCE WEDGES WITH LEMON AND DILL VINAIGRETTE

The one thing that any serving of fish and chips needs is a beautiful, crisp salad. The key to success, especially when you're not entertaining in your own home, is to keep everything as easy and fuss-free as possible, and this recipe is exactly that. To ensure your salad stays fresh and crisp, store it in an airtight container on ice in a portable cooler until ready to serve.

2 iceberg lettuces, cut into wedges

2 avocados, diced

Lemon and dill vinaigrette

3 tablespoons freshly squeezed lemon juice

1 tablespoon white-wine vinegar

60 ml (2 fl oz/¼ cup) extra-virgin olive oil

½ teaspoon dried dill

pinch of salt

pinch of ground black pepper

pinch of sugar

½ tablespoon dijon mustard

—

SERVES: 8
TIME: 15 MINUTES

Start by making the vinaigrette. Combine all the ingredients in a small bowl and whisk until emulsified. Taste and adjust the seasoning if needed. Set aside.

Place the lettuce wedges and avocado in a large bowl, drizzle with the vinaigrette and gently toss together until lightly coated.

Present your salad in a bowl or serving dish. On this occasion, I have even used printed paper cones as individual serves.

WATERMELON MOJITO

½ small, seedless watermelon, rind removed, flesh cut into chunks

1 bunch mint, leaves picked, 6 sprigs reserved for serving

1 tablespoon caster (superfine) sugar

1 lime, cut into wedges

310 ml (10½ fl oz/1¼ cups) white rum

ice cubes, to serve

–

SERVES: 6
TIME: 10 MINUTES

Purée the watermelon in batches in a blender.

Pour the pulp through a fine-mesh sieve into a measuring jug, pressing on the solids to extract as much juice as possible. You should have about 750 ml (25½ fl oz/3 cups). Discard the solids.

In a large container, combine the mint, sugar and lime wedges. Using the back of a wooden spoon, crush the mint and lime until the sugar has dissolved. Add the watermelon juice and rum and fill the container with ice cubes. Stir to combine.

Pour into individual glasses and serve with more ice and fresh mint sprigs.

VODKA-INFUSED WATERMELON

1 × 750 ml (25½ fl oz/3 cup) bottle vodka

1 large watermelon

–

SERVES: 24
TIME: 24 HOURS

To create a flat side so that your watermelon can sit upright, slice a small portion of the rind off lengthways to create a flat surface and to stabilise it. Take care not to cut into the flesh to prevent leaks.

Remove the cap from your vodka bottle and use it to trace a hole on the top-centre of your watermelon, opposite the flattened surface.

Carefully cut around the circle with a sharp knife and remove the piece of watermelon rind. This is where the neck of the vodka bottle will sit while the fruit infuses. Save the piece of rind to use as a plug for later if you will be transporting the watermelon.

Use a teaspoon to hollow out the area inside the hole so that there is room to insert the entire neck of the bottle. To test the fit, put the cap back on the bottle and insert the entire neck of the bottle into the watermelon. Make sure it can rest securely in this position.

Take the bottle out of the watermelon and remove the cap. Angle the watermelon on its side with the hole facing out so that you can clearly see where you are placing the vodka bottle. Carefully push the neck of the vodka bottle into the watermelon and straighten everything up again.

Allow the watermelon to infuse for 12–24 hours at room temperature. Once the vodka has infused into the watermelon, remove the bottle and replace the watermelon 'plug' in hole. Refrigerate until cold, then cut into slices and enjoy responsibly.

TIME TO RELAX

 After chatting, swimming and eating lunch, it will most definitely be time to lay in the sun. Set up matching beach towels so that it looks a little like a beach club, with fans and bottles of cold water at the ready. Have your beach party playlist set up with a small speaker, along with a selection of sunscreen lotions. It's time for your guests to relax in style.

SOMETHING
FOR THE KIDS

If you have invited children to your
beach party, it's fun to create some
activities for them to enjoy. Away from
the eating and drinking stations, set up
a game of beach volleyball, keep tubs filled
with a variety of balls and frisbees, and invite
your guests to join in and have some fun.

RAMADAN

A TIME TO START AFRESH

66 Ramadan is a sacred time of year in the Islamic faith. It is a month of fasting and prayer, and a time where families come together. Celebrated in the ninth month of the Islamic lunar calendar by millions of Muslims around the world, Ramadan includes fasting from sunrise to sunset and abstaining from the rituals of daily modern life, like drinking coffee, smoking cigarettes and snacking. It is a time of self-restraint and reflection to become closer to Allah, the idea being that by fasting, one understands the pain and discomfort of the poor and underprivileged.

During this month, a light meal is eaten before dawn and the fast is broken at sunset with the Iftar meal. Each night is celebrated with family gatherings and prayer. The end of Ramadan is marked with the holiday Eid al-Fitr, a time to celebrate the sacrifices that have been made throughout the month. The day of Eid represents a new month and a chance to start afresh.

THE
TABLE

 For this celebration, I embraced everything that I love about the Maghreb and Middle East. Islam is practised across many countries, in subtly different ways, and is influenced by local traditions and culture. My interpretation here represents just one of these – I have chosen to focus on the culture of a country I love to spend time in: Morocco.

In the garden, under the shade of a great oak tree, I set up a beautiful tea tent. Inside the tent, I kept the table traditionally low to the ground with my guests sitting around it. Using an oversized coffee table with masses of cushions to lounge on is a simple way to create this look. Firstly, make the ground cozy and comfortable with a big rug, and arrange your table and plenty of cushions in a relaxed fashion. Focus on colour, texture and pattern, layering as much as you can to give the space a luxurious feel.

Erected during the month of Ramadan, a tent is a place for all to gather to feast after fasting. It is a meeting place for friends and family, and although Ramadan tents are a relatively new tradition, I love the idea that, once a day, you are all gathering 'under one roof'. Inside my tent, I am decorating the table with beautiful red garden roses, tin lanterns, red grapes and halved pomegranates. Fresh mint in bunches lines the centre of the table, surrounded by collections of nuts still in the shell. Flickering candles and lanterns light the space, creating a

warm, inviting feeling. Iftar is, of course, all about the food, so the idea of sharing with friends and family means that the tagines need to have a special place on the table. Setting your plates with simple mustard-yellow linen serviettes that contrast with the deep-red place cards, roses and pomegranates ties it all together.

Everyone loves something sweet after a meal, so our special after-dinner treat (in keeping with my Moroccan theme) is coffee, tea and dates. I set up a beautiful butler's tray laden with coffee, an array of cups and a pot, fresh mint and hot water, and a lovely box of dates.

With this style of dining and décor, you really can't go wrong! It is all about colour and texture, layering fabrics and creating a look of abundance with your props. More is more, as long as you stick to three main colours with only a few shades in-between. Entertaining under the stars and enjoying a table laden with food is my idea of heaven.

EASY CHICKEN TAGINE

200 g (7 oz) chicken breast, cut into large cubes

600 g (1 lb 5 oz) chicken thighs or wings

1 tablespoon harissa paste

1 tablespoon vegetable oil

1 onion, sliced

2 garlic cloves, crushed

1 teaspoon ground cinnamon

1 teaspoon ground cumin

1 teaspoon ground ginger

1 teaspoon ground turmeric

1 teaspoon chilli flakes

450 ml (15 fl oz) chicken stock

100 g (3½ oz) dried apricots, quartered

1 × 400 g (14 oz) tin chopped tomatoes

1 × 400 g (14 oz) tin chickpeas, drained and rinsed

2 tablespoons freshly chopped mint

2 tablespoons freshly chopped flat-leaf (Italian) parsley, plus extra to garnish

couscous, cooked according to the packet instructions, to serve

150 g (5½ oz) Greek-style yoghurt, to serve

handful of flaked almonds, to garnish

—

SERVES: 4
TIME: 1 HOUR 15 MINUTES, PLUS MARINATING

Like most slow-cooking methods, a tagine is all about soaking up flavour. The conical shape of the lid draws up the steam and creates condensation, which then drips down, keeping the ingredients nice and moist – yum! Never cook in a cold tagine, they can crack. Instead, always make sure your tagine is at room temperature before you start your feast, and bring it to temperature slowly. Since the tagine creates steam as it cooks, you don't need to add too much liquid to the dish. Once cooked, the tagine can be taken straight to the table as it makes a beautiful serving dish too. Just make sure you place it on a heatproof mat to protect your tabletop.

Combine the chicken breast and thighs with the harissa paste in a bowl. Cover with plastic wrap and refrigerate for 2 hours.

Gently bring the tagine to temperature over a low heat, then heat the vegetable oil in the base of the tagine over a medium heat. Fry the chicken pieces for 2–3 minutes, then remove with a slotted spoon or tongs and set aside.

In the remaining juices, fry the onion for 5 minutes or until soft. Stir in the garlic and spices.

Return the meat to the tagine along with the stock, apricots and tomatoes. Season with salt and pepper.

Bring to the boil, then cover with the lid and simmer for 45 minutes. Add the chickpeas, cover and let simmer for a further 15 minutes.

Once cooked, stir in the mint and parsley. Serve with fluffy couscous and Greek-style yoghurt, and top with the almonds and extra parsley.

DATES – THE HOLY FRUIT

" Dates are ever-present during the holy month of Ramadan, and they feature heavily on the Iftar table – the meal at sunset that breaks fasting for the day. They are the first thing that is eaten when daily fasting is broken. Dates are easily digested and quickly satiate hunger. They are rich in natural sugars, which give a much-needed boost of energy at the end of the day.

The date palm branch is a symbol of power, triumph, abundance and faith. It is used in many religious ceremonies and festivals.

SPICE OF LIFE

Every culture uses distinct spices in their cuisine. The herbs and spices used in the Maghreb and in Middle Eastern cuisine are rich and flavoursome, and act as a fantastic base for many dishes. They include:

- Cumin
- Nutmeg
- Cardamom
- Turmeric
- Sumac
- Caraway
- Baharat
  (a combination
  of seven spices)
- Aniseed
- Allspice
- Cinnamon

VALLEY OF THE ROSES FESTIVAL

Take a six-hour drive outside of Marrakech, Morocco, and you will find the Valley of The Roses. I'm not sure anything could sound more inviting or decadent than the M'Goun Valley – or la Vallée des Roses, as it's known in Morocco. Between April and mid-May, it is said that between 3,000 and 4,000 tonnes of wild roses bloom. What a dream! Each day before dawn, roses are gathered by hand; some are sold to local distilleries to make rosewater, soaps and potpourri, but the majority are bought by big French perfume houses, for whom the M'Goun roses are most desirable.

COFFEE
READING

Coffee reading is something fun to do at the end of a delicious dinner. It is lighthearted and keeps the conversation flowing. Traditionally, coffee readers use Turkish coffee, but any coffee can be used. What you're looking at is the shape of the sediment in your cup and on the saucer.

Use a white cup so the coffee is clearly visible against the porcelain. Drink all but one sip of your coffee, then place the saucer on top of the cup. Swirl it three times in front of your chest, in a clockwise motion. Now, turn the cup and saucer upside down to allow the coffee to run down the sides of the cup. Leave the cup to sit and cool for 5–10 minutes. Pass your cup to the cup reader. The position of the coffee plays an important role in the interpretation of the symbols. You can find detailed instructions online if you are interested. 'Let the future follow your wishes,' says the interpreter of the coffee cup before the reading begins …

WHAT DO YOU SEE IN YOUR COFFEE?

◈ **Angel:** Good news and happiness are approaching

◈ **Bird:** News

◈ **Chain:** A legal union, marriage or business partnership

◈ **Egg:** Wealth and success

◈ **Eye:** Envy and jealousy

◈ **Face:** Concern for you from a loved one

◈ **Heart:** Love, faith and trust

◈ **Lines:** If a line is straight, trouble-free progress; if it's wavy, then it points out difficult progress

◈ **Ring:** Marriage; a broken ring means marriage in trouble

◈ **Star:** Journey or investment

◈ **Sun:** Power and success; a rising sun means sudden success

◈ **Triangle:** A change is coming

JEWISH
NEW YEAR

DAYS OF CELEBRATIONS

❝ If you give me an occasion, I will celebrate it.
I am lucky enough to live in Melbourne, Australia:
a diverse, multicultural city, which means I get the
chance to celebrate four or five New Years each
year, and Rosh Hashanah is one of them.

The Jewish New Year is all about honouring God's
creation of the world. The opportunity to start
afresh in a new year should be cherished regardless
of your religion. The two days of Rosh Hashanah are
a time to celebrate with friends and family, a time
of gathering for special meals, of prayers and visits
to the synagogue. Rosh Hashanah gatherings have
been held since the earliest days of the Israelites,
and it is wonderful to see and be involved in a
celebration with so much history.

With a celebration as ancient and symbolic, sharing
it with family is a must. Special family traditions
come alive at this time of year, where the young
learn from the old and, in turn, create new traditions
for their families after them.

Yom Kippur – the fast day and holiest day of the
Jewish year – concludes the High Holy Days and is a
day of asking forgiveness for the wrongdoings of the
past year and taking time for personal growth and
self-reflection.

KEEPING UP TRADITIONS

> Traditions in family life are a large part of the glue that holds us all together. As a child, it was comforting to know that Christmas or Easter was always held at Grandma's house, and that we always ate on the 'good' plates in the 'good' room just for these few select days of the year. It is this tradition that I love and would love for my children to pass on to theirs; all occasions deserve to be enjoyed in the 'good' room on the 'good' plates.

I love that the braided challah bread loaf takes centrestage at Jewish family meals. During Rosh Hashanah, the bread is formed into a circular shape. It can be made with honey or raisins and is baked during the festive season to bring joy and happiness.

THE TABLE

This beautiful, lush glasshouse filled with an abundance of green ferns is the perfect setting for my Rosh Hashanah dinner. A square table set with a patterned tablecloth and serviettes is all that is needed on this important occasion. This celebration is all about food (as are all Jewish meals), so the food has to be the hero, not the table setting.

To do something a little different, I created my own pattern for the tablecloth and serviettes and had them printed locally. This is such a great way to bring a personal, bespoke touch to a table setting. And, if you have had something designed for a particular occasion, you can use it again in the years to come, creating new traditions with your family.

I love the effect of using various shades of blue in the serviettes, tablecloth and beautiful navy and patterned china around the table. The blues and greens used throughout the space make the setting feel relaxed, informal and lush – perfect for a family meal. Silver cutlery and blue glassware complete the look.

HONEY CAKE

butter, for greasing

3 black tea bags

4 eggs, separated

220 g (8 oz/1 cup) sugar

350 g (12½ oz/1 cup) honey

250 ml (8½ fl oz/1 cup) vegetable oil

525 g (1 lb 3 oz/3½ cups) self-raising flour, plus extra for dusting

icing (confectioners') sugar, for dusting

–

SERVES: 12
TIME: 1 HOUR 30 MINUTES

Preheat the oven to 180°C (350°F). Grease a 24 cm (9½ in) bundt tin with butter and dust with flour.

Make a strong black tea by using the 3 tea bags in 250 ml (8½ fl oz/1 cup) boiling water. Allow to cool.

Beat the egg yolks and sugar in a large mixing bowl, using an electric mixer, until pale, light and fluffy. Add the honey and beat well, then mix in the oil.

In a separate bowl, beat the egg whites until stiff peaks form.

Alternating the ingredients, gradually beat the flour and tea into the egg yolk mixture. Once all combined, gently fold the egg whites into the batter. Do not overmix – you want to keep the air in the egg whites to help make the cake light and fluffy.

Pour the batter into the cake tin and bake for 50–60 minutes, or until a toothpick inserted in the middle of the cake comes out clean. Leave the cake to cool in the tin, then run a knife along the side and turn it out onto a large round plate or cake stand.

Dust with icing sugar before serving.

66 SWEET AS HONEY

Honey is such a wonderful natural sweetener. It also has a long medicinal history and can be used for skin care – that's what I call sweet!

FUN FACTS ABOUT HONEY

◈ Honey is great for your skin. It acts as a cleanser and has natural antibacterial properties that soothe and heal the skin.

◈ You can use it to moisturise your hair and scalp. Shampoos can strip your hair of its protective oils, whereas honey balances the oil production and is great for a healthy scalp.

◈ Honey doesn't spoil, so it's great in the pantry all year around.

◈ Make a natural cough syrup by dissolving 2 tablespoons of honey in a mug of boiling water, then squeeze in a little lemon juice and sip away.

◈ For minor burns, raw honey can soothe and heal the skin. It's also good for little cuts as it acts as a natural antibacterial gel.

OLD-FASHIONED APPLE CIDER

KNOW YOUR APPLES

Gala apples are very sweet. Similar to
Golden Delicious, this apple is a great all-
rounder. Granny Smiths are crunchy and tart.
A favourite with pie makers for their acidity,
this variety makes a great addition to many
recipes where some tartness is needed.
The Fuji apple is full of crunch and flavour,
making it ideal for salads and snacking.
The Pink Lady is a sweet apple with a slight
edge of tartness. Gorgeous in colour, this
apple can be used for just about anything.

HOW TO PREVENT YOUR APPLES FROM BROWNING

◈ Immediately drop freshly sliced apples into
acidulated water

◈ Soak cut fruit in ginger ale

◈ Soak cut fruit in salted water

◈ Sprinkle with ascorbic acid

◈ Wrap a rubber band around a cut apple to
hold it in its original form

60 ml (2 fl oz/¼ cup) good-quality apple cider
or juice

dash of angostura bitters

1 teaspoon brown sugar

ice cubes, to serve

60 ml (2 fl oz/¼ cup) bourbon or rye whiskey

apple slice and cinnamon stick,
to garnish

–

SERVES: 1

In a lowball glass, combine the apple cider, bitters
and sugar with a swizzle stick or a skewer. Stir until
the sugar has dissolved.

Top with ice, then add the bourbon. Garnish with
an apple slice and a cinnamon stick.

SYMBOLS OF ROSH HASHANAH

 Challah is a bread that symbolises the continuity of life. It is baked in a circular shape during the Jewish New Year, and a meal would not be complete without this offering. Made from enriched yeast dough, eggs and oil, this bread is quite easy to make and can be found in abundance in Jewish bakeries around this time of year.

Honey-dipped apples symbolise sweetness and good health. Dipping a sweet slither of apple into sweet honey is considered a way to be blessed with a sweet new year.

Pomegranates symbolise the abundance of goodness and happiness. It is said that a pomegranate has exactly 613 seeds that connect it to the 613 commandments of the Torah.

CREATIVE WAYS TO USE APPLES AROUND YOUR HOME

◈ Use them as stamps. Halve an apple and slather it with some paint to make a fun apple-shaped stamp. Perfect for making wrapping paper. Simply lay your blank craft paper down and stamp away.

◈ We all love a natural remedy. To brighten up your face, grate a peeled and cored apple and apply the flesh to your skin. Let it sit for 15 minutes, then rinse with warm water.

◈ Cut out the core of an apple and insert a tealight to create a tealight apple candle holder.

◈ Freeze apple juice in an ice-cube tray to add some sweetness to a glass of water or vodka and tonic.

◈ To accelerate ripening, place unripe bananas, avocados and tomatoes in a paper bag with an apple – it will take them from green and hard to sweet and tender in no time.

◈ Store cakes and baked treats with half an apple; the moisture from the apple keeps the cake fresher for longer. Just be sure to use an airtight container.

◈ Place a slice of apple in a sealed bag with hardened brown sugar. The sugar will be soft again in a few days as the sugar absorbs the moisture from the fruit.

DIY
SERVIETTES

Having your serviettes match your table is sometimes a little tricky. One of my favourite things to do is make my own using fabric purchased by the metre (foot). Or, on this occasion, creating and printing my own. By purchasing fabric, you can create a tablecloth with matching serviettes.

Long, flowing tablecloths that cover your table legs are perfect for dramatic dinners, and simple, long runners are great for luncheons. Choose your dining style, picture the look you are trying to achieve, and then it's off to your local fabric store.

fabric of your choice

ruler, fabric marker and scissors

fixing pins and sewing needle

thread (in a matching or contrasting colour)

—

1. Using a ruler and fabric marker, mark out even squares on the fabric at your desired size (allow extra for the napkin edge to be sewn). Cut out.

2. Place a napkin on a flat surface, patterned side down, and fold in one of the edges to form a small triangle. Repeat with all other edges. You can use fixing pins to hold things in place.

3. Fold the tip of the triangle under itself to create a straight edge. Use fixing pins if required.

4. Fold in one of the long sides of the napkin.

5. Tuck the long side in under itself to create a straight edge (you want to hide the raw edge where the fabric was cut).

6. Repeat steps 4 and 5 with all other sides, using fixing pins to hold the fabric in place. Bring the sides up far enough to create a right angle at the corners of the serviette.

7. Using a sewing machine (or by hand), stitch around the entire edge of the serviette to create a seam, using your favourite stitch.

8. Your napkin is ready! Repeat until you have the desired amount of napkins.

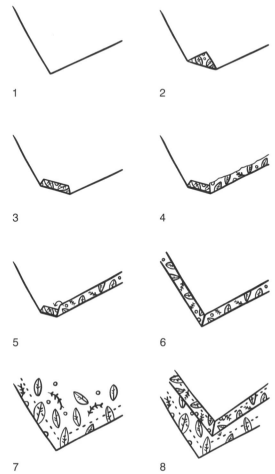

1

2

3

4

5

6

7

8

Rosh Hashanah

Chicken liver and schmaltz pate

Fish quenelles

Chicken and white wine soup with
spinach matzo balls

Prune and red wine brisket

Red and golden beet tzimmes

Spicy carrot kugel

Apple and hazelnut strudel

Apple honey cake

RAINBOW PARTY

COLOUR YOUR LIFE

" One of my greatest parenting joys was organising my kids' birthday parties. Does that come as a surprise to you? Things haven't changed much now that they're older either; I still organise their parties. A colourful rainbow-themed party is perfect for when your children are small. You can go crazy with colours, and it works for both boys and girls. Have you noticed that when kids walk into a party, their eyes immediately search out the birthday cake? So why not make your party table the best it has ever been and draw them in with colour, excitement and a rainbow full of fun? Then ply them with savoury goodness before letting them go crazy on the sweets.

“A single long table set for all the mini guests to sit at created the focal point of this fanciful rainbow party. This look is all about colour blocking and colour gradation. You want it to be in the order of the rainbow and stay consistent with actual rainbow tones. By using a white table setting and chairs, the colours pop just that bit more.

To make this long white table, I bought a piece of MDF wood and painted it in a white gloss. I used milk crates as table legs and painted them white, as well.

I bought inexpensive white stools for the children to sit on and kept the table low to cater to my guests' smaller size. An arrangement of balloons in all shapes and sizes overhead creates an amazing rainbow cloud to sit beneath.

I love the idea of an all white table with an effect in the colours of the rainbow added, setting by setting, using the paper plates, matching cutlery, serviettes and cup.

Down the middle of the table, creating an eye-catching centrepiece, a collection of Perspex letters spells out the word 'rainbow' (it could also spell out the birthday girl or boy's name). Each letter was filled with block colours of confetti in the same colour as the nearest place setting.

Another great way to create your table rainbow (and a great treat for your partygoers) is to create a colourful and bright display of sweets. Using glass vases in a variety of sizes, make a straight line down the length of the table. The vases could hold an assortment of candy, along with a collection of snacks.

INVITATION
IDEAS

When planning any event, an invitation is a must. Even in times of social media and texting, there's no excuse not to send out invites. Invitations set the mood of the party, give it a sense of formality and give a hint of the style or theme of the event. If you want your party to be taken seriously, send a paper invitation.

Hard copy invitations create a real sense of occasion and excitement when they arrive in the mail. The paper, font, colour and wording of your invitation is also important. And, if you are going to the effort of styling your home, creating a menu and serving up a fun meal, then why not make a strong first impression by sending an invitation to match?

SOME INVITATION IDEAS

◈ Lollipops with an invitation attached.

◈ A small paint palette and paint with party details painted on the palette.

◈ Pantone paint cards with party details handwritten on.

◈ A colourful spinning flower with party details on an attached gift tag.

◈ A packet of bright pencils accompanying an invite written in pencil.

◈ A simple white envelope filled with colourful confetti.

SWEET AND SAVOURY RAINBOW BUFFET

A theme is a theme, so why should the menu get left out? There are so many healthy (and not-so-healthy) treats that can be easily made to be rainbow coloured or reflect the different colours of the rainbow. The sky really is the limit with this menu, pardon the pun!

SWEET

◈ Layered coloured jelly

◈ Rainbow popcorn

◈ Rainbow meringues

◈ Rainbow pancakes

◈ Macarons

◈ Cupcakes

◈ Fairy bread

SAVOURY

◈ Rainbow triangle sandwiches

◈ Rainbow fruit or vegetable kebabs

◈ Rainbow vegetable platter (sliced vegetables in the shape of a rainbow)

◈ Rainbow Buddha bowls (mixed cut fruit strips over yoghurt)

◈ Sushi

RAINBOW PIZZA

Unfortunately, birthday parties can't be all about the cake. But that doesn't mean the main meal shouldn't be pizza! A fabulous rainbow vegetable pizza is the perfect birthday lunch. It fills little tummies with a bit of goodness before the sweet treats are devoured.

2 pizza bases

125 ml (4 fl oz/½ cup) homemade or store-bought pizza sauce

75 g (2¾ oz/½ cup) grated mozzarella cheese

600 g (1 lb 5 oz) chopped colourful raw veggies; I used broccoli florets; green, yellow and orange capsicums (bell peppers); cherry tomatoes; red onion and beetroot (beets)

2 teaspoons olive oil

–

SERVES: 8
TIME: 30 MINUTES

Preheat the oven to 220°C (430°F).

Lay out the pizza bases in a single layer on a large baking tray. Divide the pizza sauce between the two bases and use a spoon to spread it over the top.

Sprinkle the cheese on top of the pizzas, then layer the veggies in a rainbow pattern on top of the cheese. Drizzle each pizza with a bit of olive oil.

Bake for 20 minutes, or until the veggies are cooked and the crust is slightly golden. Slice and serve warm.

THE RAINBOW CAKE

This is one of my favourite cakes, both in appearance and in flavour. Any cake that is layered with cream-cheese icing (frosting) will always be a hit in my eyes. Pair that with the fluffy, buttery and moist red-velvet cake, and it's just scrumptious! I love the concept of using two cakes to create a single image. It's so simple and yet so effective, and works really well if you have a large number of guests. If you don't want to make two rainbow cakes, simply halve the recipe.

Cake batter

500 g (1 lb 2 oz) unsalted butter, softened, plus extra for greasing

575 g (1 lb 4 oz/2½ cups) caster (superfine) sugar

3 teaspoons vanilla extract

6 eggs

600 g (1 lb 5 oz/4 cups) self-raising flour, sifted

85 g (3 oz/⅔ cup) cocoa, sifted

375 ml (12½ fl oz/1½ cups) buttermilk

125 ml (4 fl oz/½ cup) natural red food colouring

Cream cheese icing

2 × 460 g (1 lb) packets cream cheese, softened

250 g (9 oz) unsalted butter, softened

900 g (2 lb) icing (confectioners') sugar

2 teaspoons vanilla extract

natural food colouring in the shades of the rainbow (red, orange, yellow, green, blue, indigo and violet)

—

SERVES: 24
TIME: 2½–3 HOURS

NOTE
For this party, I wanted my cakes to be extra tall so I doubled the recipe amount and created two cakes with four layers each.

Preheat the oven to 160°C (320°F). Grease and line two 20 cm (8 in) round cake tins with baking paper.

To make the cake batter, place the butter, sugar and vanilla in the bowl of a freestanding electric mixer and beat for 8–10 minutes, or until pale and creamy. Scrape down the sides of the bowl and add the eggs, one at a time, beating well after each addition.

Add the flour, cocoa, buttermilk and red food colouring, and beat on low speed until just combined.

Divide the batter between the two prepared tins and smooth the tops with a palette knife.

Bake each cake for 1½ hours to 1 hour 40 minutes, or until a skewer inserted in the middle of the cakes comes out clean. Leave to cool in the tin for 10 minutes before turning the cakes onto a wire rack to cool completely.

While the cakes are cooling, prepare the cream cheese icing. Combine the cream cheese and butter in a large mixing bowl of an electric mixer and beat on medium speed for 1–2 minutes, or until creamy. Gradually add the icing sugar and vanilla and mix until smooth.

Trim the tops of the two cakes so that they are flat, then split them in half horizontally with a large, serrated knife to make four cake layers. Place one cake layer on a plate and spread about a quarter of the cream cheese icing on top. Place the second cake layer upside-down on top to create a nice flat surface, then press down gently. Repeat with the remaining two cake layers and another quarter of the icing to make the second cake.

Thinly spread some more cream cheese icing over the side of the cakes to crumb-coat, then spread a generous amount on top and smooth it out with a spatula.

Take one-quarter of the remaining cream cheese icing and divide it between small bowls. Shade each bowl of icing with the different food colourings and mix well. Transfer each coloured icing to separate disposable piping (icing) bags fitted with 1.5 cm (½ in) star tips. Keep the remaining cream cheese icing plain.

Working on the side of the cake, pipe a rainbow arch using each of the coloured icings. Your rainbow should wrap around roughly one-third of the cake. Repeat on the other cake.

Once you're happy with your rainbows, fill the remaining surface area of the cake with florets of plain icing.

I'M THIRSTY!

" When it comes to the drinks at a kids'
rainbow party, you'll have to make your own
if you want to match them to the multi-
coloured theme. Using small milk bottles
and clear straws, add your drink of choice –
be that water, lemonade or soda water (club
soda) – to the bottle, then add a few drops
of natural food colouring to make the liquid
the colours of the rainbow. Fresh juice and
cordial are also great, and getting those
colours right is half the fun.

HOW TO CREATE AN AMAZING CANDY BUFFET

A candy bar works best when it's colour-blocked and abundant. When organising your candy bar, think about the number of guests you will be having, take into consideration their age, and fill your vessels accordingly.

◈ Display your candy in a collection of similar vessels. I like to use clear glass vases and food canisters in a variety of heights, surrounded by similarly coloured decorations. Vases are great – you can get the height needed for impact, and using different sizes means that you can have more of some sweets and less of others. Different levels and heights always create impact and, if you find that your vases aren't quite high enough, simply turn a shorter vase upside and place the candy jar on top. For this rainbow party, all my candies are in the rainbow palette, similar to the birthday table. Keep your plates or candy bags close at hand so your guests can fill them with their loot. Small, colourful scoops keep everything hygienic, neat and tidy.

◈ To tie back to my theme, I also created a giant rainbow made of ribbon, pom poms and paper. It made such a strong impact and is a fun thing to create with the help of the kids. If there are any leftover balloons, blow them up and let them float around the yard for the kids to play with.

RAINBOW PARTY FAVOUR

A3 sheets thick cardboard

pencil

scissors

measuring tape

hot-glue gun

glue stick

crepe paper (1 packet each of your desired colours)

Trace a circle onto cardboard using a large plate, then trace a smaller circle in the centre using a saucer. Cut out around the outer circle, then cut out the small inner circle. Next, cut the shape in half across the middle to form two arches – they'll be the sides of your rainbow.

Next, create the tops and bottoms of your rainbow. Measure the length of the top and bottom arch of your rainbow shape and cut a strip of cardboard to the required length and your desired depth (make it deep enough to fit the treats).

Measure the flat bases of your rainbow arches and the depth of the top and bottom strips and cut out two squares that match these dimensions (they will be the 'feet' to close your rainbow-shaped box).

Glue the long strip along the top of the arch, using a hot glue gun, then glue the small strip along the inside of the arch. Glue the second arch on the top, creating a rainbow-shaped box.

Glue one square onto the base of the rainbow. Now it's time to decorate.

Using a glue stick, cover the bottom arch in crepe paper (I have used blue).

Cut strips of crepe paper and fringe it. Now, have fun layering the strips from the bottom of your rainbow up.

Fill the favour with candy, then glue on the remaining square to close the rainbow and cover the foot in crepe paper. The favour can now be taken home as a gift (or it can be hung up and used as a piñata)!

PARTY GAMES

◈ Pass the parcel with different-coloured paper for each round.

◈ Hang the pot of gold on the rainbow (set this up outside on a tree).

◈ Decorate your own rainbow cupcake. This can be done at the table then taken home.

◈ Musical chairs using different-coloured rainbow chairs. Keep the balloons tied on for a crazy distraction.

◈ You can't have a party without a rainbow piñata (see opposite).

◈ Hanging rainbow doughnuts from a string and seeing who can eat theirs first with their hands tied behind their back.

◈ Rainbow treasure hunt – hiding small rainbow packets around the garden for each guest to find their specific colour.

◈ Balloon bop. Each child has to dance to music keeping a balloon in the air. If a child's balloon touches the ground, they're out.

HALLOWEEN

HALLOWEEN IS ALWAYS A TREAT

" I love any excuse to dress up my home, and Halloween is always a treat. Whether it's just for decoration or you are planning a spooky dinner party, Halloween is the perfect excuse to go a little bit silly and have a good time. You don't need to spend a fortune to create fun little treats for trick-or-treaters, but you can certainly do better than simply putting out a bowl of chocolates.

Set an afternoon aside and get crafty; a little bit of planning can go a long way, and nothing is better than seeing the smiling face of a child with a spooky treat in hand. I love the lead-up and the fact that fantastic decorations are everywhere.

A SPOOKY ARRIVAL

The entry to your home is the all-important stage for your trick-or-treater, so it needs to be the central point of your décor on this particular night. I have chosen to work solely in black and white with a pop of orange this year, and I love that almost everything I need is available at $2 shops. Collecting items such as cobwebs, fake spiders, bats, bugs and the like and littering your entrance with them sets the tone for what will be a fantastic table setting just inside the door – if you dare to enter!

Creating the right ambience for a spooky night comes down to the lighting. Dimmers, candles, flickering lights and lamps covered in fabric create the best mood lighting.

ONCE UPON A TIME ...

In the beginning, Halloween was celebrated as the Celtic festival of Samhain with the lighting of bonfires and people donning costumes to ward off ghosts. Samhain marked the end of the harvest season and the beginning of winter. It was believed that during Samhain, the souls of the dead returned to earth, and it was a time where homage was paid to the deceased. Dressing up and performing was encouraged and paid for with food.

Moving on to the eighth century, Pope Gregory III chose November 1 as a time to honour all saints, creating All Saints' Day. The evening before was known as All Hallows' Eve and, later, Halloween. Over time, Halloween evolved into the kooky, spooky night we all know and love, a night to scare away ghosts and spirits.

PUMPKIN CARVING

The European custom of 'lighting fruit' on All Hallows' Eve was said to ward off evil spirits. After carving scary faces into hollowed-out gourds and turnips, embers were burned inside them to make them glow. When the Irish settled in America, they were introduced to pumpkins. They soon realised that hollowing out and carving pumpkins was a lot easier than turnips. Faces were carved into the pumpkins and the light from the lanterns was used to light the way home.

◆ While it's fun to carve pumpkins for this special night of the year, have you ever thought about using the whole vegetables as props? With so many different sizes and varieties of pumpkins to choose from, you are spoiled for choice when using them in your home to add pops of colour. I love grouping them surrounded by tulle; the combination of orange and black is stunning, and this set-up can work anywhere in your home.

◆ If you would like to have a go at creating your own carved pumpkin, start by cutting off the pumpkin top, keeping it as a lid. Next, hollow out the pumpkin using a knife, spoon and/or any other suitable scooping tool. Carve the facial features into the front of the pumpkin (you can use a marker to draw them on and then cut along the lines to make things easier). Place a candle inside your hollowed-out pumpkin, arrange it next to your front door – done!

THE TABLE

 Once the trick-or-treaters have gone home, it's time to dial up the spook a notch with your Halloween dinner. A well-laid dinner can be the pinnacle of the night, and my plan was to make a seriously eerie dining room.

For my spooky dinner, I decided to use my lounge room. This, of course, meant rearranging the furniture and moving out some of it to create the ultimate space for this scary setting. The fireplace and bookshelves were perfect for decorating, too.

Using only lamps and candles to light the space, I kept things dark and gloomy by covering the table with black tulle. Every table needs a strong centrepiece and, for this one, I added a variety of old chandeliers for a bit of old-world ghoulish glamour. Next, I surrounded them with a collection of bones and skulls, black crows and, of course, spider webs.

I set the table with silver charger plates, black dinner plates and an eclectic mix of silver cutlery and black glassware to finish it off. When dressing a table, I always add more, then step back and review it. Mainly, I look for gaps – are there too many decorations? Does your cutlery get lost? Do you need to add another colour to the mix? Keep adding, or taking away, until you have the desired effect, and remember that when everyone is seated you want them to have space for their drinks as well as room for the food.

COCKTAIL PARTY FOOD IDEAS

All parties, regardless of their theme, should offer a selection of savoury and sweet foods. Depending on your creativity, you can go all out and theme every treat, or do what I like to do and create your traditional party finger food with a themed twist. That might involve adding food colouring to dips, changing your platters and napkins to reflect the theme, or adding props to the side of bowls, plates and glasses.

STUFFED HALLOWEEN CAPSICUMS

6 yellow capsicums (bell peppers)

4 tablespoons olive oil, plus extra for drizzling

225 g (8 oz) lean minced (ground) beef

1 onion, finely diced

2 garlic cloves, chopped

1 medium zucchini (courgette), finely diced

4 roma tomatoes, seeded and finely diced

chilli flakes, to taste

185 g (6½ oz/1 cup) cooked mixed long-grain and wild rice

185 g (6½ oz/1½ cups) grated cheese

–

SERVES: 6
TIME: 1 HOUR 35 MINUTES

Preheat the oven to 180°C (350°F).

Cut the tops off the capsicums and set aside (do not discard). Remove all the seeds and membranes from inside the capsicums, then rinse and pat dry with paper towel.

Use a small paring knife to carve jack-o-lantern faces into each capsicum. If the capsicums don't stand upright, use the knife to slice a small amount off the bottom to flatten the surface.

Heat half the olive oil in a large frying pan over a medium–high heat. Add the beef, season with salt and pepper and fry for 8–10 minutes, breaking up the lumps with the back of a spoon, until the meat is cooked through and just beginning to brown. Transfer the meat to a plate lined with paper towel to absorb any excess fat.

Wipe out the frying pan and add the remaining olive oil. Add the onion and cook for 3–4 minutes, or until beginning to soften. Add the garlic and zucchini and cook for another minute. Add the tomatoes and season with salt and a pinch or two of chilli flakes. Continue cooking until everything is heated through, then stir in the beef and the cooked rice. Taste and adjust the seasoning, then stir in 125 g (4½ oz/1 cup) of the cheese.

Fill the capsicums with the rice and beef mixture and top each with a sprinkle of the remaining cheese. Lastly, close with the reserved capsicum tops. Transfer to a baking dish and pour a small amount of water into the bottom of the dish. Drizzle the capsicums with olive oil. Cover the dish with foil and bake for 30 minutes, then remove the foil and bake for another 15–20 minutes until the peppers are starting to soften and the cheese is melted and lightly browned.

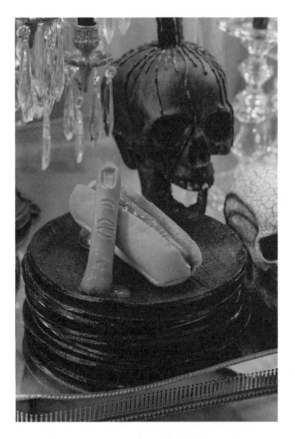

BLOODY FINGERS

12 hot dogs

12 hot dog buns

ketchup

onion, for the 'fingernails' (optional)

–

SERVES: 12
TIME: 10 MINUTES

To make the fingernails, make two incisions at the end of each hot dog to create the two sides of a fingernail, then cut another straight across the top. Make a slightly curved incision for the nail bed. Next, take your knife and carefully slice the tiny piece off.

To make the knuckles, make one incision along the middle of the hot dog with two crescent-shaped slits directly above and below. Then, halfway between the knuckle and the nail, make another two crescent-shaped slits.

Bring a large pot of water to the boil and boil the hot dogs for 4–5 minutes.

Place each 'finger' into a hot dog bun loaded with ketchup, making sure to smear some ketchup on the bottom of each 'severed finger' and more at the top of the bun.

If you want, you can add a thinly sliced square piece of white onion for the 'nail'.

MERINGUE BONES

6 large egg whites

345 g (12 oz/1½ cups) caster (superfine) sugar

–

MAKES 18
TIME: 1 HOUR 20 MINUTES

Preheat the oven to 200°C (400°F). Line two baking trays with baking paper.

Put the egg whites and sugar in the bowl of a freestanding electric mixer (make sure this bowl is heatproof). Set the bowl over a saucepan of simmering water and heat, whisking constantly, until the sugar has dissolved and the mixture feels warm to the touch, about 5 minutes.

Return the bowl to the mixer and fit the mixer with the whisk attachment. Beat on high speed for about 8 minutes, or until very stiff peaks form. Transfer the meringue to a piping (icing) bag fitted with a 1 cm (½ in) plain round nozzle.

Carefully pipe bone shapes, each 12.5–15 cm (5–6 in) long, onto the baking paper. Working in long, continuous motions, start by piping a horizontal S-shape at the top, then pipe a straight line down to form the middle of the bone, then finish with another horizontal S. Repeat until all of the meringue has been used.

Bake for about 1 hour, or until the meringue is firm but not browned. Leave to cool completely on a wire rack before serving.

CHOCOLATE CUPCAKES

Cupcake batter

230 g (8 oz/1 cup) caster (superfine) sugar

150 g (5½ oz/1 cup) self-raising flour

60 g (2 oz/½ cup) Dutch cocoa powder

125 ml (4 fl oz/½ cup) buttermilk

180 g (6½ oz) unsalted butter, softened

1½ teaspoons vanilla extract

3 eggs

Chocolate buttercream

150 g (5½ oz/1 cup) white chocolate buttons

180 g (6½ oz) unsalted butter, softened

215 g (7½ oz/1¾ cups) icing (confectioners') sugar

1 teaspoon vanilla extract

2 tablespoons milk

–

MAKES: 20
TIME: 1 HOUR

Preheat the oven to 180°C (350°F). Line a 20-hole muffin tin with cupcake cases.

Start by making the cupcake batter. In a large bowl (or the bowl of a freestanding electric mixer), sift and stir together all the dry ingredients. Add the buttermilk, butter and vanilla. Beat on low speed until just combined, then increase the speed to medium and beat for another 2 minutes. Add the eggs and beat for another 2 minutes until a smooth batter forms.

Spoon two level tablespoons of batter into each cupcake case. Bake for 20 minutes, or until a skewer inserted in the middle of a cake comes out clean. Transfer the muffin tin to a wire rack to cool for 10 minutes, then carefully remove the cupcakes from their holes and place on the rack to cool completely.

While the cakes are cooling, prepare the buttercream. (If you are making the Marshmallow ghost cupcakes, see opposite, skip this step.) Melt the chocolate buttons either in the microwave, in shorts bursts so that the chocolate doesn't burn, or in a bowl set over a saucepan of simmering water. Once melted, set aside.

Combine the butter and icing sugar in the bowl of a freestanding electric mixer and beat on low speed to combine, then increase the speed to medium and beat for 4 minutes. Add the vanilla and milk and beat for a further 2 minutes, or until the mixture is very pale and fluffy.

Add the melted chocolate to the bowl and beat on low speed until combined. Increase the speed to medium and beat for 1 minute, or until the mixture is light and fluffy. Spoon the buttercream into an icing (piping) bag fitted with a small or medium open-star nozzle.

For a classic look, pipe large swirls of buttercream on top of each cupcake while the buttercream is still soft, or follow the instructions on page 173 to create Chocolate pretzel spiders or Kooky cookie bats.

MARSHMALLOW GHOSTS

1 batch Chocolate cupcakes (opposite)

250 g (9 oz) softened butter

185 g (6½ oz/1½ cups) icing (confectioners') sugar

200 g (7 oz) marshmallow crème (fluff) or marshmallow spread

½ teaspoon vanilla extract

50 g (1¾ oz) milk chocolate buttons

–

MAKES: 12
TIME: 20 MINUTES

Prepare the chocolate cupcakes and let them cool.

Cream the butter and vanilla with an electric mixer until light and fluffy.

Add the sugar and mix until well combined. Fold in the marshmallow crème.

Transfer the mixture to a piping (icing) bag fitted with a plain, round nozzle. Pipe little ghosts on top of the chocolate cupcakes.

Melt the chocolate buttons, either in the microwave, in shorts bursts so that the chocolate doesn't burn, or in a bowl set over a saucepan of simmering water.

Dip the end of a skewer into the melted chocolate and dab two eyes onto the marshmallow ghosts. Refrigerate until ready to serve.

CHOCOLATE PRETZEL SPIDERS

1 batch Chocolate cupcakes (page 170)

1 batch Chocolate buttercream (page 170)

100 g (3½ oz) milk chocolate buttons

200 g (7 oz) white chocolate buttons

1 × 150 g (5½ oz) packet chocolate-coated stick pretzels (see Note)

—

MAKES: 12
TIME: 20 MINUTES

Prepare the chocolate cupcakes and let them cool before coating with chocolate buttercream using a spatula. You want a smooth finish for the spider body.

To make the spider legs, melt three-quarters of the milk chocolate buttons, either in the microwave, in shorts bursts so that the chocolate doesn't burn, or in a heatproof bowl set over a saucepan of simmering water. Line a flat baking tray with baking paper.

Cut or break your stick pretzel into shorter sizes for the spider leg parts. Create angled spider legs by dipping a stick pretzel into the melted chocolate and joining it with a second stick pretzel at a right angle. Place on the baking tray. Once you have created all spider legs (eight per spider!), place the tray in the refrigerator for 30 minutes for the chocolate to set.

Once ready to decorate, stick eight legs into each cupcake. Melt the white chocolate buttons. Using a piping (icing) bag with a small tip, pipe your desired number of white 'eyeballs' onto each cupcake, at varying sizes. While the white chocolate is setting, melt the remaining milk chocolate, then use a skewer to dab pupils onto the white spider eyes to finish.

NOTE
You can buy store-bought chocolate-coated pretzels, or simply make your own. Melt 200 g (7 oz) dark chocolate following the instructions in the method above. Dip the stick pretzels into the melted chocolate and set aside to cool on a baking tray lined with baking paper.

KOOKY COOKIE BATS

1 batch Chocolate cupcakes (page 170)

1 batch Chocolate buttercream (page 170)

1 × 137 g (5 oz) packet Oreos

250 g (9 oz) mini marshmallows

50 g (1¾ oz) milk chocolate buttons

—

MAKES: 12
TIME: 20 MINUTES

Prepare the chocolate cupcakes, ensuring not to overfill the cupcake cases – you want the cupcakes to remain relatively flat on top. Bake and let cool. If required, you can cut the top flat before icing the cupcake with buttercream. Use a spatula to flatten the icing across the cupcakes.

Cut the chocolate cookies in half to create semi-circle bat wings, then stick them onto the bat cupcakes.

Next, add two mini marshmallows for eyes.

Melt the milk chocolate buttons, either in the microwave, in shorts bursts so that the chocolate doesn't burn, or in a heatproof bowl set over a saucepan of simmering water.

Dip the end of a skewer into the melted chocolate and dab two pupils onto the marshmallow 'eyeballs'.

NOTE
You can use melted white chocolate buttons to further decorate the bats. For example, you could create other facial features, such as fangs.

SET UP A SPOOKY BAR

When you throw a fun Halloween party, you just have to have a dedicated drinks bar. Make the bar an inviting space and ask your guests to help themselves. Make sure you have plenty of everything so that it looks abundant, with just the right amount of spook to keep them coming back for more.

◈ Make a delicious punch full of floating oddities and display it in a great drink dispenser. This is a fun way to add some height to your bar.

◈ On an old tray, add a collection of glassware in different shapes and sizes. Place plastic spiders in each glass to spook your guests.

◈ Glass skull containers are fun to use with black and white straws, and any drink works in them.

◈ Syringes full of grenadine are so much fun, and I really think the more you add the better it looks.

DIRTY SHIRLEY TEMPLE

plastic syringe

grenadine syrup

150–180 ml (5–6 fl oz) store-bought lemon lime–flavoured soda

30 ml (1 fl oz) vodka

ice cubes, to serve

—

SERVES: 1

Fill the syringe with grenadine syrup. Pour the soda and vodka over ice in a glass tumbler and serve with the bloody syringe.

EYEBALL PUNCH

1.5 litres (51 fl oz/6 cups) mixed red fruit juice

1.5 litres (51 fl oz/6 cups) grape juice

750 ml (25½ fl oz/3 cups) soda water (club soda)

ice cubes

Blueberry ice

250 g (9 oz) blueberries (approx. 1 punnet)

Lychee eyes

1 × 425 g (15 oz) tin lychees in syrup

16–20 fresh blueberries

–

SERVES: 16

Start by making your blueberry ice.

Fill an ice-cube tray with your blueberries (chop any larger ones to fit). Fill the trays with filtered water and freeze overnight.

For the lychee eyes, drain the lychees and discard the syrup (or save for another recipe, such as the Happy Dragon Cocktail on page 38) and any damaged fruit.

Tip the lychees onto a plate or a tray lined with paper towel and gently pat dry. You should end up with about 16–20 whole lychees. Press a small blueberry into the middle of each lychee with the dimple facing up to form the pupil of the eye.

Lay the lychees out in a single layer on a tray and freeze for 1–2 hours until solid. Transfer to a freezeproof container and store in the freezer until ready to serve.

To make the punch, mix together the juices. Fill a glass drink dispenser with normal ice, blueberry ice and lychee eyes.

Pour the punch mixture into the dispenser, then top with soda water and stir gently.

THANKSGIVING

SPREAD YOUR LOVE AROUND

66 I have always loved the sentiment behind this special day. Having one day a year to sit back, relax and talk to your family about what is making you happy in life, what you appreciate and what your dreams are for the year ahead is something we don't do nearly enough. This wonderful holiday is all about giving thanks, so, whether you do this on Thanksgiving Day itself or any other day of the year, it really shouldn't matter; it's all about spreading the love.

The earliest Thanksgiving feasts were held in gratitude to the year's abundant harvest. In the United States, the first Thanksgiving was celebrated in the early seventeenth century. It was a three-day feast, and Pilgrims and Native Americans shared in the festivities. The day was formally recognised when George Washington declared it a national day of 'thanks and care' in 1789, before Abraham Lincoln made it an official federal holiday in 1863.

THE
TABLE

 What better way to celebrate nature than to set up a Thanksgiving feast in the middle of a veggie patch? I am so thankful for the variety of fresh produce we have available, so I set the table in the middle of a vegetable garden, keeping it rustic as a nod to traditional Thanksgiving.

As it's all about the garden, I just had to dress my table to suit. At my local gardening store, I found some terracotta saucers that I spray-painted in chalk paint. These acted as my charger plates, adorned with linen serviettes. I used a potting table that needed a little dressing up, so I collected baby cabbages, brussels sprouts, artichokes and asparagus to present down the middle of the table.

I have used gardening tools in table settings before – they add a bit of quirkiness to the arrangement. They're cheap and easy to come by, so think about them when planning your next outdoor party. Small black watering cans acted as my water jugs, and small spades and forks helped out as food servers. A great wheelbarrow filled with ice was the perfect portable station for drinks, and I included some empty glasses alongside it, which is always a good idea when you want to send guests the message that it's a 'help yourself' situation.

Presenting the food in this setting is so much fun – just grab furniture from your home to style your outdoor entertaining space. People are often cautious about doing this, but it's interesting to see a piece of furniture in another setting, and it adds a surprising element to your styling. Use old wooden boards and upside-down terracotta pots to raise platters to a variety of heights, and continue the garden theme by using a larger watering can as a vase, displaying fresh herbs and wildflowers.

On a day that is all about giving thanks, put some thought into where you place your family and friends. It is important to show you have thought about your guests and considered who would enjoy meeting someone new, or who might prefer to avoid a sticky situation. Embossed leather tags emblazoned with the guest's name make great place cards. They are something your guests will want to keep. If you're looking for something

with more of a gardening theme, use garden labels instead. Walk the aisles of your local gardening shop and you'll find an abundance of labels, stakes and other fun items that can easily be made into place cards. From small slate boards to copper tags, there is so much to find when you really become immersed in a theme.

A little gift for your family and friends to show that you love and appreciate them is always a special touch. You may decide to package up the table centrepiece so that everyone can take home their own jute bag full of produce. Alternatively, it might be something you have ready to go, like small terracotta pots filled with soil and a cute packet of seeds for your guests to plant, or maybe a beautiful bundle of fresh herbs from your garden, tied up with string. The options are endless.

THANKSGIVING ROASTED TURKEY

125 g (4½ oz) softened butter

1 tablespoon chopped flat-leaf (Italian) parsley

2 teaspoons chopped thyme leaves

2 teaspoons grated orange zest

5.5–6 kg (12–14 lb) turkey, giblets removed, neck reserved

6 thin orange slices

1 quantity Stuffing (page 188)

2 onions, cut into wedges

2 carrots, cut into 2.5 cm (1 in) pieces

2 celery stalks, cut into 2.5 cm (1 in) pieces

500 ml (17 fl oz/2 cups) turkey or chicken stock, plus extra if needed

Gravy

roasting juices from the turkey

3 tablespoons butter

3 tablespoons plain (all-purpose) flour

2 large thyme sprigs

1 teaspoon fresh lemon juice

–

SERVES: 8
TIME: 4 HOURS

NOTES

To truss the turkey, wrap butcher's twine around the bird's neck. Tuck the wings under its body to prevent them from burning. Hold them in place with the twine. Next, secure the twine by tying a knot under the breastplate. Cross the turkey's legs and tie them in place by firmly wrapping the twine around the bone twice and tying a knot.

For info on how to carve a turkey, see page 189.

Preheat the oven to 180°C (350°F).

In a mixing bowl, combine the butter, parsley, thyme and orange zest. Season the butter mixture to taste with salt and pepper and mix well.

Beginning at the neck end of the turkey, use your fingers to carefully make a pocket between the flesh and skin of the turkey breasts. Gently slide all but 1 tablespoon of the butter mixture into the pocket underneath the skin and carefully spread the butter to cover the turkey breasts, being careful not to pierce the skin. Slide the orange slices underneath the skin over the breasts.

Stuff the main turkey cavity with the stuffing, then truss the bird (see Note) and spread the reserved 1 tablespoon butter over the skin. Sprinkle with salt and pepper.

Place the reserved turkey neck, onions, carrots and celery in a large, heavy roasting tin. Pour 250 ml (8½ fl oz/1 cup) of the stock over the vegetables, then place the turkey on top and cover the breasts with foil.

Roast for 2½ hours, then remove the foil and add the remaining stock to the tin. Continue roasting for another 30 minutes, or until a cooking thermometer inserted in the thigh registers 80°C (175°F).

Remove the roasting tin from the oven and transfer the turkey to a platter, reserving the pan juices. Rest for 30 minutes. Remember that the turkey will continue to cook and the internal temperature will continue to rise as it rests, so don't be tempted to overcook it.

While the turkey is resting, prepare the gravy. Strain the juices from the roasting tin into a bowl. Spoon off any fat that rises to the top. Top the liquid up to make 1.25 litres (42 fl oz/5 cups) using turkey or chicken stock.

In a heavy-based saucepan, melt the butter over a medium heat. Add the flour and stir for 2 minutes, then whisk in the roasting juices and thyme and bring to simmer over a medium–high heat.

Reduce the heat to medium–low and simmer for about 15 minutes, or until the gravy thickens enough to lightly coat the back of a spoon. Stir in the lemon juice and season the gravy to taste with salt and pepper. Discard the thyme sprigs.

Serve alongside the turkey.

STUFFING

2 tablespoons olive oil

1 small onion, diced

5 garlic cloves, minced

375 g (12½ fl oz/1½ cups) brown and wild rice blend

750 ml (25½ fl oz/3 cups) chicken or turkey stock

juice of 1 lemon

1 small cauliflower head, cut into small florets

460 g (1 lb) button mushrooms, halved or quartered (roughly the same size as the cauliflower florets)

50 g (1¾ oz/⅓ cup) pine nuts

40 g (1½ oz/⅓ cup) dried cranberries

10 g (¼ oz/⅓ cup) chopped flat-leaf (Italian) parsley

35 g (1¼ oz/⅓ cup) grated parmesan

–

SERVES: 8
TIME: 45–60 MINUTES

Preheat the oven to 180°C (350°F).

Heat 1 tablespoon of the olive oil in a large saucepan over a medium heat. Add the onion and sauté for 5 minutes, stirring occasionally. Add the garlic and sauté for 1 minute, stirring occasionally. Stir in the rice and cook for 30 seconds, then pour in the stock and cook the rice according to the packet instructions.

Once the rice is cooked and tender, stir in the lemon juice. Season with salt and pepper to taste. Set aside.

Meanwhile, place the cauliflower and mushrooms on a baking tray lined with baking paper. Drizzle with the remaining olive oil and toss the vegetables until evenly coated. Season with salt and pepper.

Roast for 15 minutes, stirring once halfway through, until the mushrooms and cauliflower are tender and lightly browned. Remove and set aside.

While waiting for your vegetables to cook, heat a shallow non-stick frying pan over a low heat and lightly toast your pine nuts. Be sure to keep a close eye on them, as they tend to burn very quickly.

Combine the toasted pine nuts, rice mixture and the cauliflower and mushrooms in a bowl, then wait until the mixture has cooled to room temperature before adding the cranberries, parsley and parmesan. Stuff your turkey and, if you have any leftover stuffing that won't fit, serve it warm as a side dish.

BACON AND BRUSSELS SPROUT SALAD

juice of 1 lemon

juice of 1 orange

1 large shallot, minced

125 ml (4 fl oz/½ cup) olive oil, plus extra if needed

500 g (1 lb 2 oz) brussels sprouts, cleaned

125 g (4½ oz/1 cup) slivered almonds

100 g (3½ oz/1 cup) grated pecorino

6 rashers (slices) cooked bacon, chopped

–

SERVES: 8
TIME: 45 MINUTES

Combine the lemon and orange juices in a bowl with the shallot. Pour the oil into the bowl in a steady stream, whisking to form an emulsion (it should appear creamier and less transparent). Season generously with salt and pepper and refrigerate until ready to use.

Using a mandoline, finely shave the brussels sprouts (use the stems as a handle, then discard) into thin slices to make a slaw texture.

Add three-quarters of the almonds, cheese and bacon to the shredded brussels sprouts and toss to combine.

When you're ready to serve, toss with the dressing and sprinkle the remaining almonds, cheese and bacon over the top. If needed, add a few more tablespoons of olive oil and toss.

HOW TO CARVE A TURKEY

❖ Remove the string and place the turkey on a carving board.

❖ Remove the legs from the carcass by first loosening them a little at the thigh socket with your hands, then carve into the joints on either side, cutting through the sockets of the bone.

❖ To split the drumstick and the thigh, again loosen them, then carve into the sockets of the bone.

❖ Remove the wishbone.

❖ To cut the breast meat, cut off the wing tip then make a horizontal incision underneath the breast towards the body of the bird. Using a fork to steady the meat, carve slices of meat from the breast. Repeat the process on the other side. Alternatively, remove the breast altogether by making a horizontal incision under the breast and then cutting off the meat in one piece. Put the breast on the chopping board and cut across it. This goes with the grain of the meat and gives a smooth slice.

❖ Remove the wings in the same way as the legs, cutting through the socket where they attach to the carcass.

❖ Place the carved meat on a serving plate.

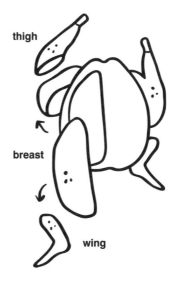

thigh

breast

wing

MAPLE BOURBON COCKTAIL

1 untreated orange

60 ml (2 fl oz/¼ cup) bourbon

30 ml (1 fl oz) freshly squeezed orange juice

15 ml (½ fl oz) pure maple syrup

1–2 dashes of angostura bitters

ice cubes, for shaking and serving

mint sprig, to garnish

—

SERVES: 1

Using a small knife, cut a thin, long strip of orange peel and twist it. Add the ingredients, except the garnishes, to a cocktail shaker and fill with ice. Shake vigorously, then strain into a rocks glass over ice. Garnish with the orange twist and mint sprig.

WHAT ARE YOU THANKFUL FOR?

To get your entire family involved in the act of giving thanks, how about creating some prompts or conversation starters? Simple words and kind gestures between family and friends can make you feel so special, and you can get the ball rolling with some activities that could turn into new family Thanksgiving traditions.

◆ After your guests have arrived, pass around pens and paper and a basket. Ask everyone to write down something they are grateful for and add it to the basket. After you have shared your meal, pass the basket around and have people randomly choose a paper to read out loud.

◆ Consider doing a round of toasts, where every guest gets to raise their glass to what they are grateful for. It can be as simple as having a roof over their heads – this exercise is all about sharing feelings with those that you love.

◆ How about creating a Thanksgiving 'awards ceremony'? Print out some fun certificates that 'thank' each guest for what they have done for themselves or others that year. Focus on them and the reasons that you are grateful they are in your life.

◆ Put your gratitude on display. Use a roll of brown paper as your tablecloth or cut it to size as placemats and let your guests jot down what they are grateful for throughout the meal. As you all sit for dessert, read the notes to each other.

◆ Create a Thanksgiving journal where every family member writes down what they are grateful for. Keep the book to be revisited, read and added to the following year – it will give you an insight into how your family has changed throughout the years.

TRADITIONAL PUMPKIN PIE

Love it or hate it, it is a staple at every Thanksgiving meal. As for me, I adore it. The sweetness of pie will always suck me in, and so too does the colour: the vibrant orange of sweet roasted pumpkin pops on the plate and can make such a statement on the table, especially if you are decorating in a traditional Thanksgiving style. Let's get baking, shall we?

Pie

2–3 sheets shortcrust pastry

140 g (5 oz/¾ cup) light brown sugar

2 teaspoons pumpkin pie spice (see Note)

½ teaspoon salt

2 large eggs

1 × 425 g (15 oz) tin pumpkin purée (or make your own)

1 × 340 g (12 oz) tin evaporated milk

2 tablespoons bourbon

Whipped cream

250 ml (8½ fl oz/1 cup) thick (heavy/ double) cream

1 tablespoon bourbon

1 tablespoon icing (confectioners') sugar

¼ teaspoon vanilla extract

—

SERVES: 12
TIME: 1 HOUR 30 MINUTES

Preheat the oven to 180°C (350°F). Spray a 23 cm (9 in) pie dish with cooking spray.

Use sheets of the short crust pastry to line the prepared pie dish. Push the pastry into the dish and trim off any excess. Use any trimmings to cover gaps in the pastry. Using a fork, prick holes all over the pastry base.

Line the dish with baking paper and fill it with baking weights or uncooked pulses. Make sure they are evenly distributed, paying particular attention to the side, as unweighted pastry will bubble.

Blind-bake for 10 minutes, then remove the weights and paper and bake for another 10–12 minutes, or until the pastry is golden. Remove and set aside to cool.

Whisk together the sugar, spice and salt in a small bowl and set aside.

In a large mixing bowl, whisk the eggs and the pumpkin purée until combined, then whisk in the spice mixture.

Gradually stir in the evaporated milk and bourbon until well combined, then pour the mixture into the pastry case.

Bake for 45–50 minutes, or until the filling has just set. Leave to cool in the dish on a wire rack for 2 hours, then refrigerate until ready to serve.

For the whipped cream, combine all of the ingredients in a mixing bowl and beat with an electric mixer until soft peaks form. Serve either on top of the pie or as an accompaniment.

NOTE
If you can't find pumpkin pie spice, simply combine 1 teaspoon ground cinnamon, ½ teaspoon ground ginger, ¼ teaspoon ground cloves, ¼ teaspoon ground nutmeg and a pinch of ground allspice.

CHRISTMAS

COMFORT AND JOY

66 Is it fair to say Christmas sneaks up on us every year? One minute it's June and then suddenly, Christmas decorations start to appear and Christmas music can be heard in every shop you walk into. Before we know it, it's all over again, and it's time to pack away the decorations for another year. Maybe it's just a sign that life is moving too quickly and we need to slow down and savour these moments? One thing I know for sure is that Christmas is the time of year I go all out to create the most spectacular family event, so I can't afford to let it sneak up on me – I need to be prepared! ·

GET ORGANISED BEFORE IT'S TOO LATE

 I don't like to be rushed at Christmas, as it makes me feel stressed instead of enjoying the holiday with my family, so I always try to get organised a couple of months in advance.

JOBS FOR NOVEMBER

◆ Make your list of guests and start thinking about the space you have and where everyone can be accommodated. If you have family staying with you, make sure all travel arrangements have been made. Diarise the amount of time you will be hosting your guest(s).

◆ Brainstorm a menu, factor in everyone's dietary requirements and email those who can help you out on the day. One person can't do everything, so try to plan it with a relative. That way, you can divide and conquer. Send those emails by the end of the month, factoring in a reminder email mid-December, closer to the big day.

◆ Make your Christmas gifting list. If you are an avid online shopper, take a few hours out of your day to shop, and keep this list handy. I don't know about you, but I always forget what I buy online (mainly because it's done late at night on the couch). Think about creating an email folder that holds all your receipts and delivery dates. If you like to venture into stores to shop, consider keeping it local. Not only are you supporting your local economy, but you don't have to fight for a car space and spend hours in a shopping centre with thousands of other people.

◆ Do a quick stocktake on your Christmas home décor. When can you get your tree? Do you need to fix any lights? Where are those stray boxes of Grandma's glass baubles? Keep everything together, so you are ready to decorate when that nominated weekend comes around.

JOBS FOR DECEMBER

◆ I always put my tree up on the first weekend of December. Put on some Christmas carols, pour yourself some bubbly and make a night of it with your family.

◆ Aim to have at least half of your Christmas shopping done by early December. You will always have a few stragglers and people you accidentally forgot, but getting the bulk of it out the way early makes December feel like a breeze.

◆ Buy a few bottles of Champagne per week. December is a month of informal pop-ins, last-minute drinks and end-of-year dinners. Keep your fridge stocked by buying a few bottles here and there. Maybe stock up on your favourites so that you have enough to get you through until New Year's.

THE CHRISTMAS TABLE

 Your Christmas table is one thing that can be set up a couple of days in advance. It's also a great way to make sure you have enough cutlery, crockery and room for everyone to sit. It's a good time to move furniture to accommodate more people and set aside the area you will be using for the bar and food. This day only runs smoothly if it's organised, so even roughly setting it up is helpful.

The masses of colour on our Christmas table were created by using the paper goods that decorated the tree and were scattered throughout the house. A colourful garland made of paper balls, honeycombs and bonbons ran down the centre of the table. For place settings, I kept it simple with a white box for every guest, wrapped in a coloured ribbon, with a contrasting laser-cut acrylic bauble featuring each guests' name. Very bright, fun and achievable.

MAKE YOUR OWN PAPER CHAIN GARLAND

◆ To make the classic paper-chain garland, visit your local craft store and pick up some packs of coloured paper (double-sided coloured paper works best, as you will see both sides of the paper).

◆ Try origami paper if you want to explore patterned chains. A 30 cm (12 in) square piece of paper will yield twenty-four 2.5 cm (1 in) × 15 cm (6 in) strips.

◆ Cut out the strips, then staple or glue the strips into rings, threading each new ring onto the last to make a garland.

◆ Alternate colours if you want a rainbow chain, or stick to one colour – it's really up to you!

DIY
CHRISTMAS
CRACKERS

 Christmas crackers are a must-have on our Christmas table. Sure, you can buy them, but this year I decided to make my own. In case you hadn't noticed, I like matchy-matchy and, seeing as my Christmas this year is a collection of block colours, I needed to make some extra-special bonbons to reflect this.

6 cardboard toilet rolls

6 sheets of wrapping paper, cut to A4 size

scissors

sticky tape

6 cracker snaps (you can find these on Amazon or other online stores)

6 mini gifts and/or jokes on strips of paper

12 × 40 cm (16 in) pieces of ribbon

–

MAKES: 6 CRACKERS

Place a toilet roll in the middle on the long edge of a piece of wrapping paper. Use a bit of sticky tape to hold it in place. Thread a cracker snap through the toilet roll and tape it down to one side of the paper.

Roll the toilet roll up in the paper, then secure the seam with a piece of sticky tape.

Tie one end with ribbon, insert a cracker gift in the open end, then tie up this end with matching ribbon. Make sure you have tied it tightly enough.

MY FAVOURITE CHRISTMAS SONGS

◈ *White Christmas* – Bing Crosby

◈ *The Christmas Song (Merry Christmas To You)*
  – Nat King Cole

◈ *Jingle Bells* – Jim Reeves

◈ *Here Comes Santa Claus (Right Down Santa
  Claus Lane)* – Gene Autry

◈ *Santa Claus Is Comin' To Town* – Perry Como

◈ *I'll Be Home For Christmas* – Bing Crosby

◈ *The Little Drummer Boy* – Harry Chorale

◈ *Rockin' Around The Christmas Tree*
  – Brenda Lee

◈ *It's The Most Wonderful Time Of The Year*
  – Johnny Mathis

◈ *Feliz Navidad* – Jose Feliciano

◈ *Frosty The Snowman* – Jimmy Durante

◈ *I Saw Mummy Kissing Santa Claus*
  – The Ronettes

◈ *Mistletoe And Holly* – Frank Sinatra

◈ *Have Yourself A Merry Little Christmas*
  – Frank Sinatra

◈ *Santa Baby* – Eartha Kitt

◈ *The First Noel* – Andy Williams

◈ *Let It Snow! Let It Snow! Let It Snow!* – Dean Martin

◈ *Winter Wonderland* – Michael Bublé

◈ *It's Beginning To Look A Lot Like Christmas*
  – Michael Bublé

◈ *Holly Jolly Christmas* – Burl Ives or Michael Bublé

◈ *Santa Baby* – Michael Bublé

◈ *All I Want For Christmas Is You* – Mariah Carey

◈ *I want a hippopotamus for Christmas*
  – Patsy Biscoe

◈ *Jingle Bells* – The Border Brass

◈ *Tijuana Christmas* – The Border Brass

◈ *Christmas (Baby Please Come Home)*
  – Darlene Love

DECORATING THE TREE

For me, Christmas is the most special celebration of the entire year, so you can probably guess that my decorations get crazier and crazier every year. I have wrapped my tree in pom poms in all shades of pink; I have kept it traditional and filled my home with miniature fir trees wrapped in glorious orange ribbons; and I have filled my tree with all the family decorations we have collected over the past 25 years. All of them perfect, all of them very special to us.

This time, we hosted Christmas, and the perfect backdrop for our tree was a wall of black bookshelves. Using a collection of paper decorations that positively popped against the dark backdrop made for the most beautiful tree. A collection of decorative honeycomb balls, streamers, tassels, bonbons, paper chains and anything else bright and fun that I could get my hands on adorned the branches, bringing an abundance of colour to what is normally a dark and serious space.

My colour palette of pink, watermelon pink, turquoise, pale blue, orange, mustard, green and rose was an absolute colour explosion. To keep the look neat, I used only block colours, no prints and patterns (with the exception of a few stripes) – just a crazy amount of colour.

I wrapped all my gifts in these block colours with contrasting ribbons, and all the decorations around the home used the same colour scheme. This is a look anyone can recreate as all my décor came from dollar shops and craft stores. You can find cheap collections that will look amazing en masse, it is just about thinking outside the box and breaking away from what is considered traditional.

QUICK TIPS FOR DRESSING YOUR TREE

◈ Get the tree looking perfect before you add the decorations. Spruce it, move the branches around, straighten them and fluff them to ensure the tree is standing tall and ready for decorations.

◈ I always put the lights on first so that they are set right back within the tree and you don't see the powers cords (your decorations will be able to cover up any unsightly cords). Ensure the lights work and are evenly dispersed around the tree.

◈ Try using a garland instead of tinsel this year. A garland will give you a strong foundation on which to base the rest of the decorations.

◈ Think about working to a colour palette. Limiting your tree to fewer colours will make it more striking and visually pleasing. Gold and silver are a classic pair, or white and silver, but even using one bold colour can create a stunning effect.

◈ Hang one set of decorations at a time. If I have a set of ornaments that are all reindeers, I will hang these up before moving on to my next style of decoration. Working sequentially like this helps to ensure that all decorations evenly cover the tree.

◈ Take a step back and admire your work from all angles. Are all the decorations evenly dispersed? Is there enough coverage? Are there any gaps? Is there too much of one particular decoration?

CHRISTMAS LUNCH

Not everything can be delegated on Christmas Day, and the cooking of the main lunch items is one of these things. I like to set up a smorgasbord of food on my kitchen bench that includes all the trimmings one would expect on this special day.

To make lunch a little less stressful, treat the day with the mantra 'many hands make light work'. Well before the day, work with your family and friends on who's going to be doing what: people in the kitchen to cook and serve, someone to pour drinks, someone to set and clear the table and someone to hand out the gifts. Whatever needs to be done on the day, there should be a designated person for that job. You should not be doing everything yourself! It is not fair that one person or a few people should be responsible for hosting and serving everyone on the day. If you are hosting the Christmas lunch, you also need time to enjoy the day.

The bright colours of my Christmas décor kept everything quite relaxed and fun, so the food presentation should also be playful. For my setting, I used a collection of different-sized white platters placed on glass vases to create the illusion of floating plates. A collection of cake stands contained the sides for the main meal, and I decorated the kitchen bench with a variety of potted Christmas trees wrapped in my chosen wrapping paper of pale blue with a green grosgrain ribbon. Behind the table, I hung a beautiful Christmas tree wall hanging to create the perfect backdrop. I decided to keep the table quite simple and clean because there was so much going on elsewhere.

PEACH-GLAZED HAM

This glaze can be made up to two days ahead. How's that for getting organised?

5–6 kg (11–13 oz) ham leg, skin removed and trimmed

Glaze

2 tablespoons olive oil

1 small brown onion, roughly chopped

2 star anise

1 teaspoon ground cardamom

2 yellow peaches, stoned and finely diced

125 ml (4 fl oz/½ cup) dark rum

125 ml (4 fl oz/½ cup) white-wine vinegar

230 g (8 oz/1 cup) dark brown sugar

–

SERVES: 8
TIME: APPROX. 1 HOUR 30 MINUTES

Preheat the oven to 200°C (400°F).

To make the glaze, heat the oil in a saucepan over a medium–high heat. Add the onion, star anise and cardamom and sauté for 4 minutes, stirring with a wooden spoon. Add the peaches and rum and continue to sauté for 5 minutes.

Stir in the vinegar and cook for 4 minutes. Add the sugar and cook for a further 4 minutes, stirring until the sugar has dissolved completely.

Remove the star anise with a fork and carefully pour the mixture into a blender, then purée until smooth.

Using a small, sharp knife, score the ham fat in a large diamond pattern. Cover the hock with aluminium foil.

Place the ham on a lightly greased wire rack in a roasting tin lined with non-stick baking paper.

Brush the glaze all over the ham, then cook for 40–50 minutes, basting with the glaze every 10 minutes, or until golden, caramelised and cooked through.

Swedish sweet-hot mustard
(*söt stark senap*)

A friend at work once gave Bruce and me a jar of this traditional mustard, referred to as *söt stark senap* in Swedish, and we just absolutely loved it. It has a different texture and flavour to our traditional English or American-style mustards. It is a little sweeter too, making it all the more delicious on a Christmas ham.

200 g (7 oz) caster (superfine) sugar

50 g (1¾ oz) honey

100 g (3½ oz) mustard powder

1 tablespoon brown mustard seeds, finely crushed

1 teaspoon white vinegar or apple-cider vinegar

–

MAKES: 350 G (12½ OZ)
TIME: 20 MINUTES

Combine the sugar and honey in a saucepan with 100 ml (3½ fl oz) water.

Heat slowly over a low heat, stirring constantly, until the sugar has dissolved, then remove from the heat and allow to cool.

When the liquid is lukewarm, stir in the mustard powder, mustard seeds and vinegar. Decant into a sterilised glass jar (see page 50), seal and rest in the fridge for 24 hours to allow the flavours to develop.

CHRISTMAS PUD'

butter, for greasing

100 g (3½ oz) pitted dates

3 tablespoons chopped crystallised ginger

zest of 1 orange

500 g (1 lb 2 oz/4 cups) mixed dried fruit, such as cranberries, cherries, apricots, sultanas and raisins

125 g (4½ oz) plain (all-purpose) flour

125 g (4½ oz) caster (superfine) sugar

150 g (5½ oz) fresh breadcrumbs

2 tablespoons brandy

handful of chopped nuts, such as pecan nuts, brazil nuts and hazelnuts

1 large, free-range egg

150 ml (5 fl oz) milk

–

MAKES: 1 MEDIUM-SIZED PUDDING TO SERVE 8
TIME: 3 HOURS 15 MINUTES

Grease a 1.5 litre (51 fl oz/6 cup) pudding bowl with butter.

Roughly chop the dates, then combine with the ginger in a large mixing bowl. Add the remaining ingredients and mix until very well combined.

Transfer the mixture to the greased bowl and cover with a double layer of aluminium foil. Tie a piece of string around the bowl to hold the foil in place.

Place the bowl in a large stockpot with a tight-fitting lid and pour in enough water to come halfway up the side of the bowl. Bring to the boil, then place the lid on the pan and simmer for 3 hours – don't forget to check the water level regularly to make sure it never boils dry. If it does, it will burn and the bowl will crack.

After 3 hours, remove the foil and turn the pudding out onto a plate. Serve warm.

THE FINISHING TOUCHES

For a garnish, I decided to make these cute gingerbread reindeer antlers. To create this look, make a batch of gingerbread dough as you normally would, then hand-cut an antler shape using a sharp knife to the size of your pud' (use your pud' bowl as a guide). Bake as normal, but be aware that if your antlers are large, they may take a bit longer to cook. Allow to cool and harden before placing on your pud'.

Salted caramel brandy butter

150 g (5½ oz) unsalted butter, softened

150 ml (5 fl oz) cold salted caramel sauce

25 ml (¾ fl oz) brandy, or to taste

—

MAKES: 300 ML (10 FL OZ)
TIME: 10 MINUTES

Beat the butter and the caramel sauce together, then add the brandy to taste, 1 teaspoon at a time.

On your work surface, roll out a sheet of plastic wrap and spoon the brandy butter down the middle. Fold in both ends of the plastic wrap, followed by one side, then roll the butter up into a log. Chill in the fridge until ready to serve.

WHY DO WE EAT CHRISTMAS PUDDING?

❖ We have been eating and enjoying plum pudding for around 300 years. Luckily, it no longer contains meat. Medieval predecessors of today's plum pudding were made from mutton and beef mixed with raisins, currants, prunes, wine and spices. Quite a difference to the sweet puddings we know today and enjoy with lashings of custard and cream. The Christmas pud' has long been a traditional family cake enjoyed at this special time of year.

❖ The pudding was also an emblem of English patriotism throughout the 1900s. Bakers were encouraged to buy their ingredients from English-owned manufacturers and then make the pudding as a way of supporting the British Empire. It made use of dried fruits when fresh were unavailable. During World War II, when rationing meant that ingredients for things such as Christmas puddings were scarce, parcels containing dried fruit, spices and suet were sent from Australia to relatives and charity recipients in England, helping to keep the tradition of Christmas pudding alive.

❖ Make your pud' months ahead and store it to give the flavours plenty of time to develop. Come the big day, it will be perfect!

TREATS
FOR SANTA

" *Sprinkle this reindeer food outside tonight,
the moonlight will make it sparkle bright.
As the reindeer fly and roam,
this will guide them to your home.*
(Source unknown)

It's that heartwarming last little job, right before bedtime: putting the treats out for Santa. I loved watching my children do this; they took their job so seriously, really trying to work out what kind of snack Santa would like and how he had room for it all (he does eat at every home, after all). It is such a beautiful tradition, so let's make sure it looks as impressive as the rest of your Christmas décor. This year, rather than leaving out a carrot and a glass of milk, why not go a little gourmet for old Saint Nick? Perhaps he would enjoy a homemade gingerbread cookie or mince pie washed down with a delicious glass of milk or a sneaky glass of port.

And don't forget treats for the old reindeers. I like to make mine extra special by mixing bird seeds with edible glitter. It's a cute gift to make and give to friends, plus it looks gorgeous sparkling away in your front garden or driveway. Just make sure the glitter is edible in case the local birds decide they want a taste.

A NIGHT-BEFORE-CHRISTMAS BOX

In the lead-up to the big day, excitement levels rise and it is just the most joyful time of year. Treating the kids on Christmas Day is one thing, but how about a little mid-week surprise to hype the kids up for the big day? You don't have to go crazy, but this is the only time of the year you can get away with wearing Christmas-themed pyjamas, so let's embrace it!

◆ Christmas-themed pyjamas, DVDs, books and some candy are perfect for filling your box. Surprising kids – or anyone for that matter – with little treats along the way just adds to the excitement. It's such a cute thing to open the night before Christmas and can start a lovely family tradition. Enjoy the last of the Christmas box goodies on Christmas night, sitting together in Christmas pyjamas, drinking a hot chocolate and watching a favourite movie.

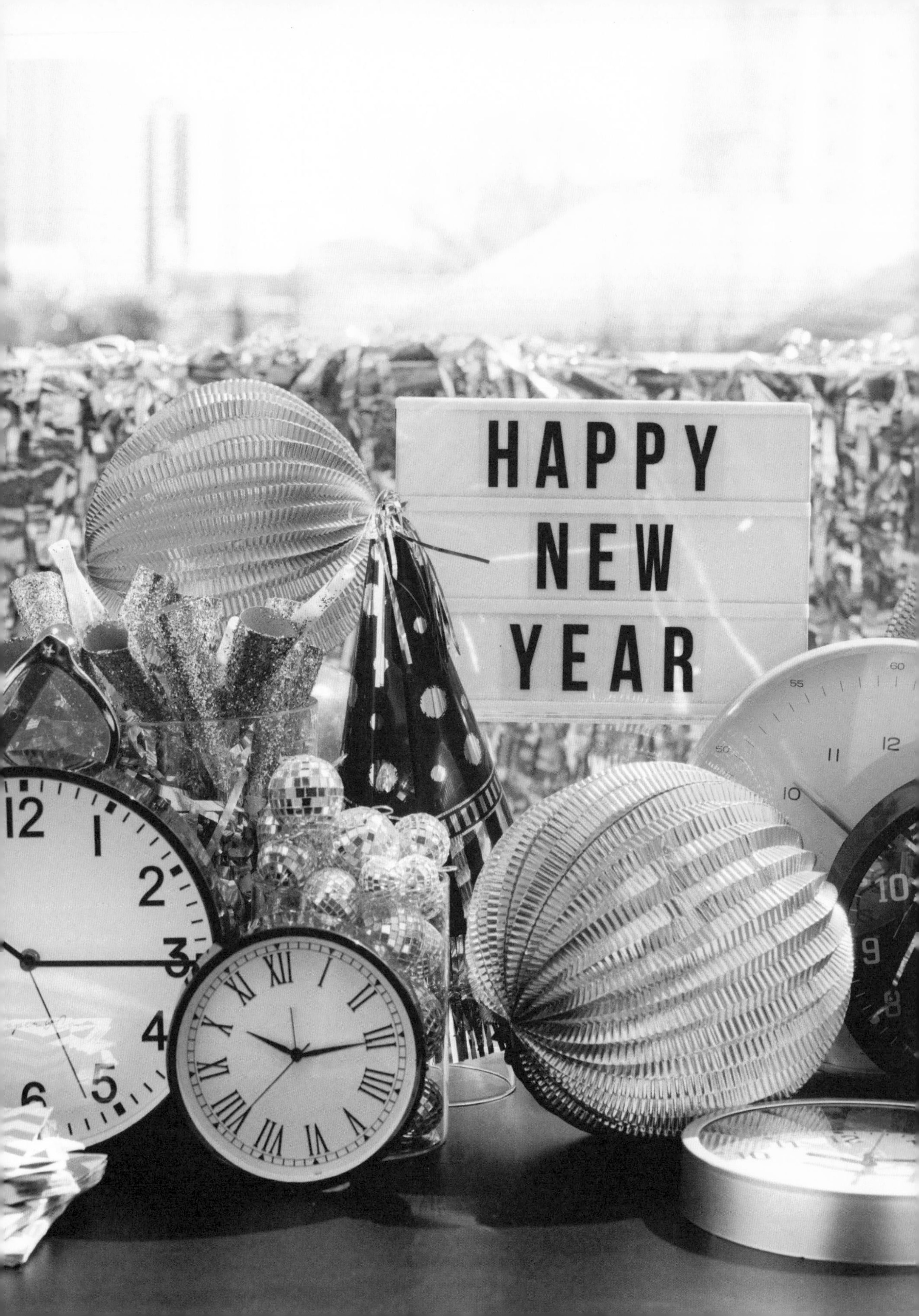
HAPPY
NEW
YEAR

NEW YEAR'S EVE

NEW YEAR'S POSSIBLITIES

> " New Year's Eve is *the* night for celebration. Whether you choose to go all out and have a large party or have a simple, intimate get-together, a night of fun and frivolity is guaranteed.

For me, New Year's Eve is all about reflecting on the past year – the good and the bad. I focus on making changes that will benefit me as well as my family. They're not resolutions as such (because who sticks to those anyway?), but small, achievable steps towards making our lives just that little bit easier, slower and relaxed in the year to come.

NEW YEAR'S EVE COCKTAIL PARTY

Personally, I love to hold a cocktail party on New Year's Eve. No matter what event you host, you'll want to feel relaxed and involved in the celebration, and a cocktail party is perfect for that. Creating a bar area means that your guests can help themselves, and a rotation of pre-prepared canapés will keep everyone snacking happily. The best part? All of this can be done with just a little preparation. Set up the bar with ice buckets and glasses, and keep it simple with Champagne, wine, beer and one special cocktail. Keep your canapés simple, and make sure there's plenty of them. Cold platters also work well, as they can be prepared in advance.

SMOKED SALMON BLINIS

150 g (5½ oz/1 cup) plain (all-purpose) flour

250 ml (8½ fl oz/1 cup) full-cream (whole) milk

125 g (4½ oz/½ cup) butter, melted, plus extra for greasing

110 g (4 oz) smoked salmon, cut into small strips

125 ml (4 fl oz/½ cup) crème fraîche

30 g (1 oz) caviar (black salmon roe)

–

MAKES: 35 BLINIS
TIME: 30 MINUTES, PLUS 30 MINUTES RESTING TIME

Combine the flour, milk, melted butter and a pinch of salt in a mixing bowl and whisk to combine. Refrigerate for 30 minutes to rest.

Preheat a large frying pan or griddle over a medium–high heat and brush with a little melted butter.

Dollop tablespoons of the batter into the frying pan (as many as will fit in the pan without touching each other). After 1–2 minutes, small air bubbles will begin to appear on the surface of the blinis. Flip them over and cook until the edges are firm and the undersides are brown. Transfer to a plate lined with paper towel. Repeat with the remaining batter. Allow the blinis to cool completely.

When you're ready to serve, top the blinis with a strip of smoked salmon, then a small dollop of crème fraîche, and finish with some caviar. Serve with plenty of sparkling wine.

FRENCH 75

 Creating a Champagne cocktail is a no-brainer for New Year's Eve. There is nothing better than being able to toast your loved ones at the stroke of midnight, so make sure you do it with something pretty in your hand.

60 ml (2 fl oz/¼ cup) dry gin

1 teaspoon caster (superfine) sugar

15 ml (½ fl oz) lemon juice

ice cubes, for shaking and serving

150 ml (5 fl oz) brut Champagne

–

SERVES: 1

Combine the gin, sugar and lemon juice in a cocktail shaker with ice and shake well.

Strain into a Champagne saucer over ice, then top with Champagne.

THE COUNTDOWN

" The highlight of New Year's Eve really is the countdown to midnight. A fun theme for this event is based on the countdown itself; by using clocks as decoration, you can have a lot of fun.

Collect all the clocks you can and start decorating with them. I took some off my walls, borrowed some from friends and family, and went to my local bargain shop for the rest. Try using the surface of a clock as a serving platter, or use smaller clocks to decorate trays. Bring a little glamour to the night by focusing on metallics and black. Silver and gold streamers create a strong statement behind the bar, and I also love using large gold helium balloons to say Happy New Year, as it's an excellent backdrop for photos and videos, which I know we are all slightly obsessed with!

MAKE YOUR SPARKLING SPARKLE

200 g (7 oz) glitter in your choice of colour

large paper plate

sheet of newspaper

6 mini sparkling wine or Champagne bottles (don't worry about removing labels; they will get covered in glitter)

spray adhesive glue

30–40 cm (12–16 in) ribbon (in a complementing colour to the glitter)

6 straws, to match the glitter (optional)

–

MAKES: 6

 I love the look of these glitter-covered bottles. Not only are they super simple to make, they also look fabulous in any colour and can be used as a fun decorative item for a party. My ultimate New Year's Eve colour palette is glittering gold, silver and black, and this is one of the few times of the year that I don't mind being covered in glitter.

Empty the glitter onto the paper plate.

Place your bottles on a sheet of newspaper. Spray the outsides, except for the bottlenecks, with glue.

Roll them in the glitter until thoroughly coated, then leave to stand for 1 hour to dry. Once dry, shake off any excess glitter and tie a ribbon around the top of the bottles before attaching a straw, if desired.

CELEBRATING
WITH CHAMPAGNE

Every celebration should be toasted with a glass of sparkling, and it's far more traditional than you might think. Evidence of sparkling wine dates back to the fifth century, and our favourite fizzy drink actually started life as a communion wine in the region of Champagne, France. Over centuries, Champagne evolved and became popular among the social elite.

And, let's face it, its popularity has never waned. Thanks to the power of advertising, Champagne quickly became the drink of choice for celebrations, particularly at Christmas and New Year's Eve.

CREATING A SPARKLER MOMENT

Hand your guests fun party favours in the lead-up to midnight. Even better, have a table set up with items such as sparklers, party hats, whistles, bright, sparkly poppers and streamers for everyone to grab when the clock strikes twelve. You can fill clear vases with these items and put them on display – that way, your guests will know they are in for a good night. Whatever you do, don't let midnight pass without celebrating – hug everyone in the room, sing a favourite song and share some Champagne.

NEW YEAR'S EVE AROUND THE GLOBE

 How about eating twelve grapes that represent the stroke of midnight just like the Spanish do? If you can eat all twelve grapes by the time the clock finishes striking twelve, you will be rewarded with a year of prosperity. A fun tradition from Denmark is to stand on chairs and jump off them as the clock strikes twelve – quite literally a leap into the new year! Then there's jumping waves in Brazil, eating a lucky seven, nine or twelve meals in Estonia, ringing bells in Japan – each country has its own traditions on this special night of the year. Let's work towards making our own unique traditions to celebrate with friends and family!

MAKE A WISH

One of my favourite New Year's Eve traditions is the Russian custom of writing out your wish for the year to come on a piece of paper, then burning it before midnight to make the dream come true. You could even save these wishes and look at them the following New Year's Eve, holding yourself accountable for the promises you made.

66 What is all the fuss about this song?

Auld Lang Syne is a Scottish poem written by Robert Burns in the late eighteenth century, sung to the tune of a traditional folk song. It is sung all over the world, especially in Western countries, to bid farewell to the old year at the stroke of midnight on New Year's Eve. It also pops up at a few other events – as a celebratory song at funerals, graduations and as a farewell or ending to other occasions. So, cheers to the new year!

Auld Lang Syne

Should auld acquaintance be forgot,
and never brought to mind?
Should auld acquaintance be forgot,
and auld lang syne?

And surely you'll buy your pint cup!
and surely I'll buy mine!
And we'll take a cup o' kindness yet,
for auld lang syne.

We two have run about the slopes,
and picked the daisies fine;
But we've wandered many a weary foot,
since auld lang syne.

We two have paddled in the stream,
from morning sun till dine;
But seas between us broad have roared
since auld lang syne.

And there's a hand my trusty friend!
And give me a hand o' thine!
And we'll take a right good-will draught,
for auld lang syne.

CHORUS:
For auld lang syne, my dear,
for auld lang syne,
we'll take a cup of kindness yet,
for auld lang syne.

INDEX

SUPPLIER CREDITS

VENUES

Flowers Vasette
flowersvasette.com.au

Glasshaus Nursery
glasshaus.com.au

Graham Geddes Antiques
grahamgeddesantiques.com.au

Mount Macedon Peonies
mountmacedonpeonies.com

Ormond Collective
ormondcollective.net.au

FOOD & BEVERAGES

The Big Group
thebiggroup.com.au

Bird In Hand
birdinhand.com.au

Koko Black
kokoblack.com

Popstic
popsticicecream.com.au

Sisko Chocolate
siskochocolate.com

Smashed Pinata Cakes
smashedpinatacakes.com.au

The Sugar Florist
sugarflorist.com.au

Sugar Rush by Steph
sugarrushbysteph.com.au

Torello Farm
torellofarm.com.au

FURNITURE

Canvas and Sasson
canvasandsasson.com.au

DANN Event Hire
danneventhire.com.au

The Design Depot Hire
thedesigndepot.net.au

Harry The Hirer
harrythehirer.com.au

Lost In LA
lostinla.com.au

Provincial Home Living
provincialhomeliving.com.au

TABLEWARE

All Fired Up Pottery
Socials: @allfiredup.pottery

Minimax
minimax.com.au

Mud Ceramics
mudaustralia.com

Place Settings
placesettings.com.au

Robert Gordon
robertgordonaustralia.com

Simmons Linen Hire
simmonslinenhire.com.au

PROPS & DÉCOR

Bits and pieces to go
bitsandpiecestogo.com

Coote&Co.
cooteandco.com.au

Florabelle Imports
florabelle.com.au

Marble Basics
marblebasics.com.au

Nomadic
shopnomadic.com

Poppies For Grace
poppiesforgrace.com

Spooktober
spooktober.com.au

Sunnylife
sunnylife.com.au

SIGNAGE

Q Signs and Showcards
qsignsandshowcards.com

Sketch & Etch
sketchandetch.com.au

Wojo Signs
wojosigns.com

ABOUT CHYKA

Chyka Keebaugh is a businesswoman, events styling powerhouse, social media butterfly and proud mother of her two children. She established events and hospitality companies The Big Group, The Design Depot and Capital Kitchen with her husband, Bruce, and for the last 25 years, they have created unforgettable events for private and corporate clients.

Chyka was the homemaking/styling expert on *Good Morning Australia* for four years and also starred in three seasons of *The Real Housewives of Melbourne*.

Home is one of Chyka's favourite places, and making it inviting and comfortable is her idea of bliss. As editor-in-chief of her online magazine, Chyka.com, she shares practical advice and tips on homemaking and entertaining guests, along with recipes and DIY projects. In 2018, Chyka released her first book, *Chyka Home – Seasonal inspiration for a life of style*, a guide to making a beautiful home all year round.

THANK YOU

Writing, styling and photographing this book has been so much fun. Each chapter was lovingly planned and created with lots of detail, different locations, colours ... But I couldn't have done it without the help of so many amazing people!

To my Mum and Dad, for allowing me to shoot on their beautiful property. It is so wonderful to have your garden come alive in the Easter and Birthday chapters of this book.

To Eliza and Damien, thank you for welcoming us into your beautiful garden. The green oak tree has always been a favourite, and I'm so happy to have used it in my Ramadan shoot.

A huge shout out to the amazing team in The Big Group kitchen for helping me get the food looking perfect, and for allowing me to be so incredibly annoying with my attention to detail.

To the suppliers and incredible people in the events industry who have lent me everything from chairs, plates, venues and decor, to props and ice creams; thank you for your help with this book.

To Flowers Vasette, you are the most incredible florist. A huge thank you for allowing me to use your laneway and flowers for my Valentine's shoot. I love the look of this chapter and it wouldn't have been the same without your incredible team and their support.

To Dann Event, Harry the Hirer and The Design Depot; you guys are the best in the industry and all your different chairs, tables and bits and pieces brought the shoots to life.

To the amazing Bronte, who truly is the person that keeps me on track. Your dedication, loyalty and love is so incredibly special to me and I feel so very blessed to have you in my life every day.

To the wonderful Shannon, who has helped me transcribe all of my words so perfectly. Your sense of humour, help and guidance on shoot days is just the best and I love how easily we work together.

To the team at Hardie Grant – this has been such a fun project, and I have loved getting to know you all better during the many shoots. How lucky have we been with that weather!

To Gavin Green, you have been such a calm and easy person to work with. The shoots have worked out perfectly, and you've captured every chapter so beautifully. I really hope we work together again soon.

It's hard to believe that my two furry mascots in *Chyka Home* are no longer with me. They are missed, but the new star of the show, Otto, has loved gracing the pages of this new book.

And lastly to my family – Chessie and BJ, you don't live in Australia anymore, but that hasn't stopped me sharing with you all of what I have been doing and getting your opinions. I greatly value your thoughts, so thank you so much.

Brucie ... well, I wouldn't have been able to do any of this if we weren't a team. We started this journey nearly 30 years ago and I love how incredibly supportive you have always been. I value your opinion more than anyone else's, so thank you for just being you.

Published in 2019 by Hardie Grant Books,
an imprint of Hardie Grant Publishing

Hardie Grant Books (Melbourne)
Building 1, 658 Church Street
Richmond, Victoria 3121

Hardie Grant Books (London)
5th & 6th Floors
52–54 Southwark Street
London SE1 1UN

hardiegrantbooks.com

A catalogue record for this
book is available from the
National Library of Australia

NATIONAL
LIBRARY
OF AUSTRALIA

Celebrate
ISBN 978 1 74379 566 8

10 9 8 7 6 5 4 3 2 1

Publishing Director: Jane Willson
Project Editor: Anna Collett
Editor: Andrea O'Connor @ Asterisk & Octopus
Design Manager: Jessica Lowe
Designer: Michelle Mackintosh
Photographer: Commission Studio
Stylist: Chyka Keebaugh
Production Manager: Todd Rechner
Production Coordinator: Mietta Yans

Colour reproduction by Splitting Image Colour Studio
Printed in China by Leo Paper Products LTD.